KIDS AND KINGDOM

KIDS AND KINGDOM

The Precarious Presence of Children
in The Synoptic Gospels

A. James Murphy

☙PICKWICK *Publications* · Eugene, Oregon

KIDS AND KINGDOM
The Precarious Presence of Children in The Synoptic Gospels

Pickwick Publications
An Imprint of Wipf and Stock Publishers
199 W. 8th Ave., Suite 3
Eugene, OR 97401

www.wipfandstock.com

ISBN 13: 978-1-62032-568-1

Cataloguing-in-Publication Data

Murphy, A. James

    Kids and kingdom : the precarious presence of children in the Synoptic Gospels / A. James Murphy

    viii + 148 p. ; 23 cm. Includes bibliographical references.

    ISBN 13: 978-1-62032-568-1

    1. Children—Biblical teaching. 2. Bible. Gospels—Criticism, interpretation, etc. I. Title.

BS576 M87 2013

Manufactured in the U.S.A.

CONTENTS

ACKNOWLEDGMENTS

THIS WORK WOULD NOT have been possible without the sacrifices, dedication, patience, and commitment of my wife, Cynthia; many thanks to you. I also thank my ten-year-old daughter, Hannah, for whom I continued to help with homework, shuttle to swim, coach her basketball team, and frequently walk to school and back. Thanks to my soon to be four-year-old daughter, Laura Claire, who sometimes crawled circles around my office chair and tried to reach up for the keyboard many times as I first began this project. I must now also acknowledge my infant son Connor who arrived at the manuscript preparation phase of this project. It will be years before any of you will understand what I have tried to accomplish here. In each of you, I shall live on long after my own days are gone.

In addition, I want to express my sincere thanks to Gregory Robbins and Pamela Eisenbaum of the Joint Program at the University of Denver and Iliff School of Theology as well as Nicholas Rockwell of the University of Denver for their insights, feedback, and enthusiasm for this project. Special thanks go to Dr. Robbins whose mentoring and numerous readings of the developing manuscript have helped it take shape. Thanks to my present institution, South Dakota State University, including the Department of History, Political Science, Philosophy & Religion for their support while I finalized and edited the present manuscript. Beyond these professionals I also wish to thank Dr. Bonnie Miller-McLemore of Vanderbilt, whose timely reconsideration of her own earlier work confirmed for me that I am not alone in finding problems with the presentation of children in the Gospels. Thanks to Mark George of the Joint Program at DU/Iliff from whom I first learned of the recent scholarship in child studies and the Bible. Finally, I wish to thank Christian Amondson, Christopher Spinks, David Belcher, Matthew Stock, and the entire editorial and design teams at Pickwick Publications, whose efforts and suggestions have only enhanced the project. Nevertheless, any shortcomings in this work are my own.

ABBREVIATIONS

CIL	*Corpus Inscriptionum Latinarum*
ILS	*Inscriptiones Latinae Selectae*
LCL	Loeb Classical Library
LS	Liddell and Scott, *A Lexicon, Abridged from Liddell and Scott's Greek-English Lexicon*
TDNT	*Theological Dictionary of the New Testament*

CHAPTER ONE

LET THE YOUNG CHILDREN COME TO ME

> Jesus loves me, this I know, for the Bible tells me so.
> Little ones to him belong. They are weak but he is strong.
> Yes, Jesus loves me. Yes, Jesus loves me. Yes, Jesus loves me.
> The Bible tells me so.[1]

THIS CHRISTIAN HYMN IS learned by countless children every year. It underscores Jesus' concern and commitment for children in the vulnerability of youth. The theme central to this hymn probably stems, in large part, from the widely familiar biblical refrain, "Let the young children come to me" (Mark 10:14 and parallels).[2] This verse has been used to justify infant baptism and communion for young children, Sunday-School programs, children and youth ministries, mission trips and Christian relief agencies that specifically target children abroad, as well as the simple practice of bedtime prayers. Some of these have only emerged in recent centuries as the Industrial Age began to alter the place and functions of children in modern western culture. Corresponding to these social changes, children and childhood have seemingly become more important in our society, and have gained significant legal protections. And yet, their prominence in the Gospels has only recently received noteworthy consideration, perhaps as an inevitable result of such changes.[3]

---

1. Lyrics by Anna Bartlett Warner (1827–1915) and William Batchelder Bradbury (1816–1868), public domain.

2. All English translations are my own unless otherwise noted.

3. Some of these changes and our altered expectations of, and demands on, children are reflected in chapter 1, "Depraved, Innocent, or Knowing: History Reinvents Childhood," in Miller-McLemore, *Let the Children Come*, 1–23.

Furthermore, like the hymn above, modern theologians and Christian writers who reflect on children, faith, and community usually reinforce our belief, perhaps *our need to believe*, that God is good and just, and is especially so where the concerns of children in all their vulnerability lie. Much of this belief is constructed by *reading* children into the creation account of Genesis 1, where God calls everything "good." For example, David Jensen has written that as creator God's benevolent justice extends to "all children, regardless of heritage."[4] Marianne Thompson explains that, "Because they are created by God . . . they have status, dignity, and inestimable value."[5] Certainly from Torah, God's concern about, and legal recognition of children, at least Jewish boys, is signified by circumcision, a mark symbolizing their covenant relationship with Israel's god, including "the youngest in the fold, even those young (such as slave children) who might be considered 'outsiders.'"[6] Still, most theologians who write on children, like Thompson, express the universality of divine concern: "God is the giver of all life and . . . the law of God protects those to whom God has given life."[7] However, such sweepingly positive assessments gloss over texts such as the flood narrative (Gen 6–9) and passages of the conquest of Canaan (Deut 20:14, 16–17) where Israel's god sentences to death untold children under circumstances not of their own making.[8] Nevertheless, with such positive assessments of the deity's concern for children, it should come as no surprise that Christian writers find the same level of concern for children in Jesus. And where the Jesus of history appears thus concerned in the Synoptic Gospels, even

---

4. Jensen, *Graced Vulnerability*, 4.

5. Thompson, "Children in the Gospel of John," 204. Another prime example of the optimistic assessment of God's universal love of children is argued in Towner, "Children and the Image of God," 307–23. Elsewhere I have responded, "Although I would rather agree entirely with these assessments, my readings of the text do not permit me to share their optimism" (Murphy, "Children in Deuteronomy," 7n23).

6. Jensen, *Graced Vulnerability*, 2. Jensen notes the limitation to male infants, yet the quote conveys his entire general tone. In other words, for Jensen, "*[The god of Israel] loves the little children, all the children of the world*" (Murphy, "Children in Deuteronomy," 7n26).

7. Thompson, "Children in the Gospel of John," 204.

8. Murphy, "Children in Deuteronomy," 14. Among the small number of scholars who have begun to write on these problematic texts in the Hebrew Bible, see Fewell, *Children of Israel*; P. Miller, "That the Children May Know," 45–62, especially 58–61; and Fretheim, "God Was with the Boy," 3–44; Fretheim, "God, Abraham, and the Abuse of Isaac," 49–57.

more so the post-resurrection Jesus of faith, petitioned as God throughout the Christian world for protection and sustenance.

As I write these words, my one-year-old daughter studies me from her high chair; my eight-year-old stands proudly next to me in our picture from last year's father-daughter dance. From these faces I recall how god-like my own parents once seemed to me at a tender age. Caregivers such as parents or guardians feed and clothe us; they can seem omnipresent in our early lives. They can mete out god-like punishments that in pre-adolescent years seem unchallengeable. And they provide a sense of unrivaled security, and may even be called upon to display such protection before their child's eyes. A faith is developed within the child, a faith in the god-like provisions of her caregivers.[9]

So what then becomes of such faith when the god fails? How does the child's perception of his or her father (or *Father*) change when protection is suddenly needed and is not forthcoming? Maybe the father or mother is absent, or perhaps the perpetrator of some act against the child. Of course we mortal caregivers are not gods, and sometime ago, usually in our adolescence, we learned that neither were our own caregivers.

Fortunately for many, the Hebrew Bible makes it pretty clear that the god of Israel is not human, and the New Testament points toward the divinity of Jesus as his son. Furthermore, a number of scholars claim that Christianity has been directly responsible for positive steps in the concern for and treatment of children throughout history.[10]

Still, what happens within a child when her faith, and the god of her faith, fails to protect and provide against all that threatens? Matthew says the risen Christ promised his followers (usually taken implicitly to include

9. This "faith" seems akin to what modern child cognitive development researchers call "attachment." Modern research on child development confirms what seemed intuitive in ancient sources about children, that is, their dependency on adults. In the words of cognitive scientist Alison Gopnik, childhood is "a distinctive developmental period in which young human beings are uniquely dependent on adults. Childhood couldn't exist without caregivers." To survive, it is incumbent upon them from infancy to learn to make and interpret attachments in order to develop healthy social and cognitive behavior. By one year of age, children recognize some people treat them differently than others; these people are looked to for the process of forming attachments. Babies (and presumably young children) "pay particularly close attention to the contingencies between their own actions and emotions and those of others—the statistics of love" (Gopnik, *Philosophical Baby*, 10, 180–81).

10. For example, Ronning, *Jesus and the Children*. I shall describe Ronning's views in the survey of literature. See also Wiedemann, *Adults and Children*, esp. chapter 6; Bakke, *When Children Became People*; and Horn and Martens, *Let the Little Children Come*.

Christians today), "And remember, I am with you always, to the end of the age" (28:20b; NRSV). Yet, where is God for the untold numbers of children of every generation suffering abuse or neglect? Where is Jesus for the thousands of victims of sexual abuse by priests, church leaders, and laypersons, which has scandalized the modern Church? Lest anyone think this merely a Catholic problem, how absent the deity must have seemed for the Pentecostal boy I knew as a child that was fondled by an older member of our church. Sexual abuse knows no denominational boundaries. If the Synoptic authors[11] felt it so important to show Jesus' concern for children that he embraces them and wants them near to him, at what point does his concern languish? Is not at least one possible interpretation by one of "these little ones," represented in this paragraph, that he or she has been abandoned by Jesus? Do the Synoptic authors only present Jesus as a "friend of little children,"[12] or might they unwillingly reveal traces of a lesser god, the potential for an interpretation most "believers" would find impossible, sacrilegious, or objectionable?

In this work, I shall argue that the inclusion of *non-adult children*[13] in the kingdom of God presented in the Synoptic narratives[14] is tempered by images of household disruption and alienation of children as a consequence of Jesus' eschatological gathering of followers depicted in these three

---

11. By "Synoptic authors" I mean those authors, writers, or compilers responsible for the basic extant canonical form of the Gospels. This study does not involve forays into redaction or source criticism.

12. This phrase is borrowed from an essay title by Barton, "Jesus-Friend."

13. By *non-adult children*, I refer to those below marriageable age, especially those still dependent on the adult world around them. A more precise definition will be given in my discussion of terms for children.

14. This study examines Matthew, Mark, and Luke as distinct literary narratives in their basic extant form. Of course, textual variants that have an important bearing on this study of children will be noted. However, I am less interested in the redactional history of the texts for this project. Matthew or Luke's use of Mark or the hypothetical Q source is not as important here as how each Synoptic author portrays the relationship of non-adult children to Jesus and the advent of his eschatological kingdom *in its final form*. I have deliberately chosen not to examine the portrayal of children in John. This has nothing to do with claims to historicity for either the Synoptics or John. In John "children" seldom appear. It is used as a term by Jesus for his adult disciples (13:33; 21:5), as a term for all included in God's eschatological family (1:12; 11:52), for descendants of Abraham or the devil (8:39, 41), and for the healed royal official's son (4:49). Of these, only 4:49 seems a possible reference to (in narrative) an actual dependent boy. For this reason, John is less helpful for a study of non-adult children. However, there are some literary parallels in the Gospel of Thomas (22, 46) to certain Synoptic verses that might prove fruitful for exploration.

gospels. In fact, the Synoptic authors offer a more troubling—even vexing—vision with respect to young children, where concern for them (and other marginalized peoples) is embedded in narratives whose elements (themes, plot, sayings), when more closely scrutinized, signal enormous potential for the detachment of bonds between children and caregivers.

I begin chapter 1 by defining critical terms such *non-adult children*, *discipleship*, and *kingdom*, and explain my methodological approach. Second, I give a brief overview of the presence of children, *during the ministry of Jesus*, in the Synoptic Gospels. Since I am interested only in how children are depicted in relation to the portrayals of the adult Jesus, the birth narratives are not examined under this thesis. Third, I review the history of childhood studies and its specific history related to research in the Gospels. I round out chapter one by outlining the remainder of this study.

Terms

Before discussing method, it is paramount to define my use of certain terms critical to this study, beginning with my use of the term *children*. Wherever I use the term children, *non-adults* are implied unless explicitly stated otherwise. As much as possible, this definition must cohere with notions roughly contemporary with the first century.

Since children were so marginal in antiquity, and because almost all written material preserved from antiquity was penned by adult men, references to children and childhood are comparatively meager. The paucity of references to children in ancient sources makes determining the precise point of transition between "childhood" and "adulthood" a challenge. One of the best examinations of the complexity of the problem for antiquity is provided by John Boswell in *The Kindness of Strangers*, who chose to view children as distinguished largely by age and development:

> "Child" is itself not an uncomplicated term. Among modern writers, conceptions of "childhood" have varied widely, posing considerable lexical problems for investigators. Even the bases of distinction change: sometimes the root concept arises from chronological boundaries (to age twenty-one, to age seven, etc.), sometimes from associated aspects such as innocence, dependency, mental incapacity, or youthful appearance.[15]

15. Boswell, *Kindness*, 26.

But is it reasonable to expect such precise demarcations when our own present American treatment of children is so confusing? For example, at age sixteen we can legally begin to drive a vehicle, view movies restricted to adults (rated R) at seventeen, take up arms, kill, and die in legal combat at eighteen, drink alcohol anywhere from eighteen to twenty-one, depending upon state law, and complete a four-year college degree to embark upon adult career choices around age twenty-two. Increasingly, American judicial systems are prosecuting children ever younger as adults; and these are just social markers.[16] At what point then does childhood end and adulthood begin? If modern American social cues suggest the distinction is unclear, should we expect less when looking for children in antiquity? With this precaution in mind, we turn to a lexical examination of the various words used for "child" by the Synoptic authors.

The Greek terms used for "child" by the Synoptic authors are several: παῖς, παιδίον, βρέφος, τέκνον, υἱός, and a term in Mark for childhood, παιδιόθεν. The Greek terms for "children" in the Synoptics include: παῖς, παιδίον, τέκνον, υἱός, σπέρμα, and ἄτεκνος.[17] Beginning with βρέφος, among the Synoptics used exclusively by Luke, the term refers particularly to a "small child" or "infant."[18] παῖς, and its diminutive παιδίον, can mean "boy," "girl," "daughter," or "maiden." In certain contexts it can refer to a young age, and Hippocrates specifically distinguished παῖς chronologically, as a boy of seven to fourteen, from παιδίον (a child under seven), and from μειράκιον, an "adolescent" between fourteen and twenty-one years of age.[19]Especially in the Synoptic Gospels, forms of παῖς can also refer to infants (Matt 2:16) and physically developing children (Matt 17:18; 21:15; Luke 9:42).[20] With these terms in particular, context is important in determining whether the term is used to designate an actual child character, an adult, a slave that may or may not be a child, or is used metaphorically.

16. Biological markers, from which several social markers take their cue, are scarcely dealt with in this project. However, as I began editing this chapter, there is an Associated Press report just out on a ten-year-old Romanian girl who just gave birth in the city of Jerez de la Frontera, Spain ("10-year-old gives birth in southern Spain," http://www.9news.com/rss/story.aspx?storyid=161328).

17. Also, the term νεότης is used to designate the youthfulness of the rich young ruler.

18. Oepke, "παῖς," *TDNT* 5:637–39.

19. Ibid., 5:637.

20. Ibid. The term can hold the connotation of descent rather than age, or of social position, e.g., a slave.

τέκνον is used almost exclusively as a term of *descent*, rather than of age. Yet, since it can refer to an adult *or child* descendent (son or daughter), it cannot be excluded without contextual clues, if any, to aid interpretation. And finally, θηλαζούσαις refers specifically to nursing infants (Mark 13:17 and par.).

In addition to these terms, there are a handful of other words used by the Synoptic authors to refer to a child. Matthew uses the genitive plural form of μικρός (10:42), which may or may not refer to actual children.[21] In addition to παῖς, other terms can be found explicitly for "girl": κοράσιον (the daughters of Jairus and Herodias), παιδίσκη, and παιδίσκη τὶς (both forms refer to the servant-girl that confronts Peter during Jesus' trial). In terms of age, υἱός, "son," can be used to designate an adult (e.g., Matt 20:20, Mark 2:5 and par., and Luke 7:12), or a youth (Mark 9:17 and par.). The term for daughter, θυγάτηρ, can similarly refer to an adult (Luke 13:16) or a youth (e.g., Mark 5:34–35 and par., 6:22 and par., 7:26, 29 and par.). The terms θυγάτριον, "little daughter," and νύμφη, "daughter-in-law," are more suggestive of their respective age ranges.[22]

Social rituals can also signify the threshold between childhood and adulthood, such as marriage, becoming fully responsible for Torah observance by Jewish boys, and trading the *bulla* for the *toga pura* by boys in Roman culture.[23] However, these will be discussed more fully in chapter two where I detail the world of Jewish and Greco-Roman children in order to provide context for the characterization of children in the Synoptic Gospels. For now, let me summarize by stating that for the present work, *non-adult children are largely defined in physically developmental and social terms as those who have not yet "come of age," but particularly with those still dependent on the adult world around them.* This encompasses a period ranging from birth to roughly the mid teens.

Second, the term *discipleship* is used in this study to *describe the way of life that characterizes followers of Jesus as portrayed by the Synoptic authors.* This raises several questions that have been fully addressed by other scholars, which could easily overwhelm the present work. What characterizes a

21. This debate, mentioned in the exegetical section on Matthew, will be treated in chapter 4.

22. The most detailed examinations of these terms related to the New Testament and early Church are in chapter four of Müller, *In der Mitte*, 165–200, and Boswell, *Kindness*, 26–39.

23. On the latter see Seneca, *Epistulae* 4.2; Cicero, *Ad Att.* 5.20.9; Ovid, *Fasti* 3.777.

follower of Jesus? Do the Gospels present similar requirements for follow-ing Jesus, or do they differ? If so, how?

According to Ernest Best, the Markan form of discipleship is charac-terized by continuous movement, to follow Jesus "on the Way," a path of suffering that leads to death and resurrection, which in turn leads back to the path of service to mission.[24] It is to "deny oneself," i.e., who you are or think you are, and accept the likelihood you will be killed (therefore, *take up the cross*).[25] Not everyone who hears Jesus or encounters him takes up discipleship. Crowds frequently follow Jesus in Mark, but Jesus typically reveals certain teachings privately to a narrower group of followers than the crowds.[26]

In Matthew, the concept of *discipleship* is a bit more complex, since Matthew clearly draws on earlier material shared with Luke, and yet writes for a later audience. As it stands, Matthean discipleship includes everyone that has chosen to follow Jesus (8:21; 9:14; 10:25, 42; 12:49; 27:57; 28:19),[27] yet the *act of following* involves two dimensions for the author: 1) a call to spread the Gospel through humility and service to others,[28] and 2) ethical

24. According to Best, Mark "uses verbs of motion more frequently than any of the other evangelists" (Best, *Disciples*, 4–7, 14–15; the quote is from ibid., 4).

25. "But how is their discipleship defined [in Mark]? First, that they should come after Jesus, deny themselves and take up their crosses (8:34). It is appropriate that this definition should be given in the presence of the crowd; it is necessary to say what it means to be a disciple to those who are not disciples before . . . those who are shown to have failed to understand. The three commands, 'come, deny, take up,' here in the aorist tense indicating something which is done once and for all, are again appropriate in an address to the crowd. They are followed by a command in the present tense 'follow me' indicating a continuing attitude. Thus we have three initial actions succeeded by a process, 'keep on following.' 'Come after me' is a general command which specifically links discipleship to Jesus; *discipleship is not just the readiness to suffer, howbeit in ever so good a cause*; it is a step to fall in behind Jesus, and no other, in the way in which he is going. *The call is not one to accept a certain system of teaching, live by it, continue faithfully to interpret it and pass it on*, which was in essence the call of a rabbi to his disciples; nor was it a call to accept a philosophical position which will express itself in a certain type of behavior, as in Stoicism . . . It was a call to fall in line behind Jesus and go with him" (Best, *Disciples*, 7–9; my emphasis).

26. Albright and Mann believe Mark makes a clear distinction between disciples (those whom Jesus divulged matters to more privately) and the crowds of listeners (Albright and Mann, *Matthew*, lxxvi–lxxvii). In the previous footnote, Best sees 8:34 as a blurring of this distinction, but on the whole argues discipleship is a strenuous and costly call that probably limited its pool of adherents.

27. Boring, *Matthew*, 102.

28. Grams, "Not 'Leaders,'" 114–25; Penner, "Revelation," 209.

adherence to Matthew's community, a "messianic community, the eschatological people of God," who are believers in Christ.[29] This latter dimension provides an ironic twist, perhaps due to Matthew's incorporation of older source material. One follows Jesus (discipleship) as a member of the Matthean *community*, but living the Matthean ethical standard and evangelizing outsiders might entail relinquishing marriage, family,[30] property, and one's life (19:27–30; 24:9–10).

For Luke, *discipleship* carries a much broader emphasis than in Mark and Matthew, yet the costs of discipleship to oneself and one's relationship to family, friends, culture, and possessions seem even more severe in Luke. First, Luke deliberately broadens discipleship to include those who simply "believe" that Jesus is the savior of humanity, referring even to a crowd as disciples (6:17; 19:37–40).[31] More than any Synoptic author, Luke accepts

29. Boring, *Matthew*, 98–99.

30. In the Hellenistic world of the first century, the term most synonymous with our present word "family" was οἶκος ("household"), which according to Aristotle consisted of three principal relationships: husband-wife, parent-child, and master-slave (Aristotle *Politica* 1.3; cf. 1 Esdras 5:1). Since in this study I am more interested in the relationships between persons than non-animate possessions, I have chosen to use "family" to more narrowly convey this grouping of relationships, where "household" still retains a sense of non-animate possessions. Still, we should be careful not to separate the relational aspect of families from the fact that they were the basic unit of economic production in society. Various authors have offered definitions for the familial structure of the period. One of the most detailed categorizations for the period is Emmanuel Todd's *Seven Family Types: absolute nuclear, egalitarian nuclear, authoritarian, exogamous community, endogamous community, asymmetrical community,* and *anomic family* (Todd, *Explanation*, 19–32). Santiago Guijarro lists four different types of families for first-century Galilee based on social stratification: the *Large Family, Multiple Family, Nucleated Family,* and *Scattered*. The *Large Family* consists of a father and mother, unmarried children, and married sons with their families. The *Multiple Family* consists of two or more married families. A *Nucleated Family* consists of a father and mother, one or two sons, and some extended relatives. He describes the fourth category, which he calls *Scattered*, as "hard to tell" (Guijarro, "Family," 58). James Jeffers defines "family" within the categories of *Roman, Hellenistic, Jewish,* and *Christian* (Jeffers, *Greco-Roman World*, 238–41). Others variously define the family in quite Aristotelian terms as consisting of father and mother, parents and children, masters and slaves; some include extended kinship and lineage. A sampling includes Stambaugh and Balch, *New Testament*, 123; Osiek and Balch, *Families*, 41–42; Moxnes, "What is Family?" 21; Lassen, "Roman Family," 104–5; Ferguson, *Backgrounds*, 65. For the present work, the term "family" should be understood as somewhat fluid, but essentially anchored in a household containing a *paterfamilias* and wife/mother, married sons and their families, whether under the same roof or not, unmarried children, and slaves (Murphy, "Family Values," 11–13).

31. Albright and Mann, *Matthew*, lxxviii–lxxix.

the inclusion of marginalized and other ethnic groups.[32] However, Joseph Fitzmyer finds three demands of Lukan discipleship, once one has responded to the call of faith and conversion: 1) following Jesus in his Way, on his path to the Father; 2) prayer, which provides a sustaining connection with the Father; and 3) the follower of Christ must divest oneself of all material possessions.[33] Following Jesus leads to temporal danger, self-denial, suffering and the perpetual threat of martyrdom.[34] Although Alan Culpepper finds in Luke a wide array of characters that express joy and praise God in response to seeing the power of God at work through Jesus "and hear the good news of the kingdom,"[35] I do not think it follows that all who hear or are touched by the good news become followers.

To summarize, a common denominator to *discipleship* among the Synoptic authors is agency; discipleship involves *the ability to actively choose, or accept* the call, to follow Jesus on a path that reorients one's life toward service to others, and to proclaim a message that will likely result in persecution, perhaps death, for an otherworldly reward. Within the narratives, one who is healed by Jesus,[36] gives him food or shelter,[37] or hears his teaching might be a sympathizer, but this does not automatically translate into discipleship. Such persons could easily remain within a less sectarian strand of Judaism, at least in these gospels.

Third, without succumbing to the debate over realized or futurist eschatology, the term *kingdom* will be used to describe *the fictive realm marked by the status of "insider" in relationship to the figure of Jesus, as portrayed by the Synoptic authors.* For instance, in Mark, temptation can prevent one from entering the kingdom (9:47; cf. Matt 18:6–9), and an adult must become like a child to enter (10:15; Matt 8:3; Luke 18:17). There is an ethical dimension to this kingdom (Mark 12:34). In the words of Dennis Duling: "It is present to those who in contrast to the outsiders understand and follow Jesus, that is, those who love the one God and the neighbor as

---

32. du Plessis, "Discipleship,"64–65.

33. Fitzmyer, *Luke*, 241–51. Also see Culpepper, *Luke*, 27.

34. du Plessis, "Discipleship," 63–70.

35. Culpepper, *Luke*, 29.

36. E.g., Matt 8:1–4 or 8:5–13. In the latter pericope, the centurion is said to have faith that Jesus can heal his son. Matthew never suggests that the centurion then becomes a follower of Jesus.

37. E.g., Jesus' reprieve in the home of Martha and Mary (Luke 10:38–42).

oneself, who are childlike, and who resist temptation."[38] For Matthew, the temporal kingdom is the teachings of Jesus, which must be accepted. In order to enter, one must humble himself or herself (Matt 18:3–4), and hold to a strict ethical standard that will "bear fruit" (7:16, 20). It is a realm that suffers violence (Matt 11:12), and in Matthew is made up of both righteous and unrighteous until the final judgment (Matt 25:31–46). Finally, in Luke the kingdom is present in the midst of Pharisees who do not recognize it (17:20–21); it is the temporal visitation of the Son of Man to humanity (17:22–37). Luke also places ethical demands on those who wish to enter it, including selling one's possessions. Leaving family and home for its sake will be rewarded (18:18–30).

In conclusion, the *kingdom*'s temporal presence is manifest in and through Jesus, his teaching and works. To enter it, one must accept his teachings, abide by an ethic that subverts conventional social norms, and proclaim the gospel to others. Yet, it appears porous or fluid; some who are in it will not pass muster in the final judgment. At times, even the status of "the Twelve" can be questioned in relation to the kingdom (Mark 10:13–16 and par.).[39]

Method

I must strongly emphasize that what follows is an interpretation. Doubtless, several interpretations are possible. The texts are read as story, not history; therefore, I treat them entirely as literary productions, and only in their final form. Furthermore, I do not read these texts as stories about Jesus. Here, they become stories about children. Despite their treatment as literary productions, the Synoptic authors create them with a social world that has a basis in the *realia* of contemporary Jewish and Hellenistic-Roman family life, which necessitates the historical investigation provided in chapter two.

Why is another interpretation of Jesus' blessing of the children or his teaching about greatness in the kingdom needed? Have not others demonstrated that these passages illustrate Jesus' deep concern for children? For children, surely the clearest interpretation is that, like other socially marginalized groups in the first century, their lowly status is reversed. They are, in fact, central to Jesus' new kingdom. But if the children in these

38. Duling, "Kingdom," 56–57.

39. Ibid., 56–59. See also Albright and Mann, *Matthew*, c–cv.

stories could watch the narratives unfold, not knowing the ending ahead of time, and not privy to the ecclesiological concept of salvation history, what would they see? Would they see a movement of men and women who were really interested in them?

What follows is a deconstructive literary analysis of the Synoptic texts. As a mode of interpretation, Barbara Johnson provides a concise definition of deconstruction in a very instructive essay:

> [A deconstructive reading] is a careful teasing out of the conflict-ing forces of signification that are at work within the text itself. If anything is destroyed in a deconstructive reading, it is not mean-ing but the claim to unequivocal domination of one mode of sig-nifying over another . . . It makes evident the ways in which a text works out its complex disagreements with itself . . . [It] is first and foremost a way of paying attention to what a text is doing—*how* it means not just *what* it means.[40]

My deconstructive interpretation will be very much in keeping with Johnson's definition. By *deconstructive literary analysis*, I mean a careful examination of how parts of the text are constructed to create meaning, then dismantling the textual structures to show loci of ambiguity, where the authors attempt the illusion of a coherent text, and fall short. Although Jacques Derrida is credited with deconstruction's origination, he refused to consider it a method.[41] Characterized more as a mode of interpretation, or a particular form of critical reading, that confronts efforts toward uniform and governing interpretations, there is no clear-cut form of deconstruction.

Some scholars have attempted formulaic approaches for deconstruc-tive readings evocative of a method. For instance, Vincent Leitch asserts that Derrida's basic strategy for deconstructive reading is:

> [R]epeat and undermine. The conventional repetition of the text, minutely and laboriously accomplished, establishes the foothold of deconstruction within the resources of the text and the tradi-tion. The subversion of the text, predicated on the rich possibilities

40. B. Johnson, "Teaching Deconstructively," 140–41.
41. Derrida, "Letter," 3. See especially Derrida, *Of Grammatology*.

of textuality and intertextuality,[42] makes insecure the seemingly stable text and tradition through the *production* of undecidables.[43]

Similarly, Leitch describes J. Hillis Miller's strategy as a cautious marking and replication of certain elements in a text by the interpreter that may include its figures, concepts, or motifs. By such repetition, "the critic unleashes the disruptive powers inherent in all repetition" which shows the text to be unstable by "calling into play a disorienting chain of substitutions and displacements."[44] Returning to Johnson, she succinctly illustrates how one approaches quickly a decentering of the hierarchical relationships of power just described through a meticulous examination of the following: 1) *"ambiguous words,"* 2) *"undecidable syntax,"* 3) *"incompatibilities between what a text says and what it does,"* 4) *"incompatibilities between the literal and the figurative,"* 5) *"incompatibilities between explicitly foregrounded assertions and illustrative examples or less explicitly asserted supporting material,"* 6) *"obscurity,"* and 7) *"fictional self-representation."*[45] With particular attention to some of Johnson's examples, I now turn strategies of deconstructive reading onto narrative claims in the Synoptic Gospels.

By claiming that people marginalized by the temporal world are included as full participants in Jesus' kingdom, some interpreters would suggest that the Synoptic authors attempt to establish an "unequivocal domination" of one characteristic of the kingdom of God over claims to the contrary. Yet, such domination is not confined merely within the text.

42. In certain cases, intertextual readings will be important for highlighting the constructedness, and therefore the artificiality, of certain texts under examination. On the development and processes of intertextuality, see Hays et al., *Reading the Bible,* and Fewell, *Reading Between Texts,* particularly the essays on theory by Timothy K. Beal and Peter D. Miscall in the latter.

43. Leitch, *Deconstructive Criticism,* 177–78.

44. Ibid., 195–96. Miller describes the process of deconstructive reading in his own words as: "1) Deconstruction as a mode of interpretation works by a careful and circumspect entering of each textual labyrinth. The critic feels his way from figure to figure, from concept to concept, from mythical motif to mythical motif, in a repetition which is in no sense a parody. It employs, nevertheless, the subversive power present in even the most exact and unironical doubling. 2) The deconstructive critic seeks to find, by this process of retracing, the element in the system studied which is alogical, the thread in the text in question which will unravel it all, or the loose stone which will pull down the whole building. 3) The deconstruction, rather, annihilates the ground on which the building stands by showing that the text has already annihilated that ground, knowingly or unknowingly. Deconstruction is not a dismantling of the structure of a text but a demonstration that it has already dismantled itself" (J. H. Miller, "Steven's Rock," 341.

45. B. Johnson, "Teaching Deconstructively," 140–48.

As Danna Fewell and David Gunn note, it can also be established by the reader.

> We believe that most readers are driven to form interpretations that offer an encompassing, comprehensive, and coherent account of their text. Critical theory, in particular feminist and poststructuralist (particularly deconstructionist) discourse, helps us to see that this ["unequivocal domination" (to insert Johnson's term)] is hardly inevitable or innocent. It places a premium on sameness (unity) and univocality (one meaning), and it devalues difference (diversity) and multivocality (multiple meanings). It leads to our ignoring or suppressing the very tensions and fractures in texts that may offer us enlivening insight or, indeed, an escape from the tyranny of a given interpretive tradition.[46]

However, a deconstructionist reading of the Synoptics will show there is some literary dissonance between the claims of child inclusivity by the Synoptic authors and their portrayal of Jesus' eschatological gathering in its temporal context.

Deconstruction helps the reader to exploit such literary dissonance, to show that *there are claims to the contrary* within the text. As Timothy Beal states:

> In every text there are traces of that which has been excluded or repressed (Derrida has called them erasure marks), or even of that which is altogether absent. Indeed, a text's boundaries of meaning are always established through exclusion, repression, and marginalization. But traces remain. When attended to, these traces open beyond the narrow confines of the particular text and into relation with other texts. Traces lead readers to stray into the margins and off the page.[47]

As much as the Synoptics want to claim children as their ultimate model of the radical inclusiveness of the kingdom of God, "traces of other 'truths' . . . flicker across the surface of the text, creating enough of a disturbance to keep a perfectly unified image from stabilizing."[48] If children are models of discipleship, or are symbolically adopted into Jesus' eschatological gathering,[49] then modern interpreters of the Synoptic Gospels, I

46. Fewell and Gunn, *Gender*, 16.

47. Fewell, *Reading Between Texts*, 24.

48. Fewell, "Deconstructive Criticism," 126.

49. See Derrett, "Why Jesus Blessed," 1–18. Gundry explores Derrett's analysis further

argue, need to consider more fully the presence of children in the text. It is not a matter of errant readings. Rather, it is a question of who or what, as an interpreter, I have chosen to bring out of the margins of the text, in this case, children. A deconstructive reading permits this interpretive maneuver because it presupposes that texts have multiple voices and meanings (multivocality), and allows marginalized voices to challenge dominant voices in the text. The result is a reading that challenges interpretations that understand Synoptic portrayals of Jesus to have "liberated" children or granted them full participation in the kingdom of God.

In order to bring this interpretation into view, I shall apply a deconstructive literary reading to the texts, teasing out incompatibilities between assertions or illustrative examples that the authors explicitly foreground, and what the text actually does or leaves undone, the dissonance between the figurative and what is possible at the literal level will be tested.[50] Such a reading will enable me to foreground the tension between the Synoptic authors' claims of the radical inclusion of children in Jesus' eschatological gathering, and where the narratives fall short of these claims. Looking more closely at certain passages bearing on the cost of discipleship to families, which highlight the itinerant nature of the movement, and at themes of abandonment in the passion narratives, I shall read with children foregrounded, particularly over eschatological claims. Where the Synoptic authors emphasize a concern for children, they will be examined in light of these more problematic passages. However, the full force of the deconstructive reading cannot be brought to bear on the passages about children until I have: 1) described some of the *realia* of late Jewish and Hellenistic-Roman family life from which we may reasonably assume the Synoptic authors drew upon when constructing the social worlds of their narratives (chapter two); and 2) begun a close reading of the narratives to show how the Synoptic authors attempt to convince us that children are fully included among the followers of Jesus and within the kingdom of God; how they and family matters are straightforwardly embedded by the authors (chapter three). Only after having established this background can I begin to show how the text dismantles itself.

---

and concludes: "Jesus' hug, therefore, can be seen as an adoptive embrace, *an assumption of a parental role* (emphasis mine). His subsequent blessing indicates that he has adopted the children in order to pass on an inheritance to them before he dies, and in this way 'save' them" (Gundry, "Children," 156).

50. B. Johnson, "Teaching Deconstructively," 140–45.

Occurrences of Children in the Synoptic Gospels

Non-adult children turn up almost everywhere in the Synoptic Gospels.[51] Mark, the shortest and probably earliest of the extant gospels contains the fewest such references. Arguably, non-adult children appear in the following narratives in Mark: the restoration of Jairus' daughter (Mark 5:21–24, 35–43; Matt 9:18–19, 23–26; Luke 8:40–42, 49–56),[52] the dancing daughter of Herodias (Mark 6:17–29; Matt 14:1–12), the Syrophoenician woman's daughter (Mark 7:24–30; Matt 15:21–28),[53] a boy with a demon (Mark 9:14–27; Matt 17:14–18; Luke 9:37–43), the child set in the midst of the disciples (Mark 9:36–37; Matt 18:2–5; Luke 9:47–48), as "little ones" one must not hinder or despise (Mark 9:42; Matt 18:6–7; Luke 17:2; cf. also Matt 18:10–14), children brought to Jesus for blessing (Mark 10:13–16; Matt 19:13–15; Luke 18:15–17), children abandoned by caregivers for the sake of the kingdom (Mark 10:29–30; Matt 19:29; Luke 18:28–30), the absence of children in the resurrection (Mark 12:18–25; Matt 22:23–33; Luke 20:27–40), as victims of the cost of discipleship to households (Mark 13:12; Matt 10:21; Luke 21:16; also Mark 13:17; Matt 24:19; Luke 21:23), and perhaps finally in the form of the servant-girl who confronts Peter in the courtyard of the high priest (Mark 14:66–69; Matt 26:69–72; Luke 22:56).[54]

However, Matthew's addition of an infancy narrative, some additions exclusive to Matthew, and material shared only with Luke, can make the presence of children in Mark seem trifling. Again arguably, non-adult children appear in Matthew in the following narratives: the infancy narrative (Matt 1:18–2:23, including the story of Herod's massacre of Bethlehem's

---

51. I have deliberately chosen not to examine the portrayal of children in John. This has nothing to do with claims to historicity for either the Synoptics or John. In John child characters seldom appear. "Children" is used as a term by Jesus for his adult disciples (τέκνον, 13:33; παιδίον, 21:5), as a term for all included in God's eschatological family (τέκνον, 1:12; 11:52; and υἱός, "sons of light," 12:36), for descendants of Abraham or the devil (τέκνον, 8:39; γεννάω 8:41), for the youth who provided the five barley loaves and two fish to feed the multitude (παιδάριον, 6:9), and for the healed royal official's son (παιδίον, 4:49; υἱός, 4:46, 47, 50, 53). Of these, only the latter two seem possible references to (in narrative) an actual dependent boy. For this reason, John is less helpful for a study of non-adult children. However, there are some literary parallels in the Gospel of Thomas (22, 46) to certain Synoptic verses that might prove fruitful for exploration.

52. Matthew refers to her father only as a synagogue ruler. He is Jairus in Luke.

53. Matthew refers to the mother as a "Canaanite woman."

54. Matthew has two servant-girls confront Peter in the courtyard of Caiaphas. In Luke's version, Peter retorts, "Woman, I do not know him," (22:57), making the servant-girl's identification as a non-adult child in Luke unlikely.

infants), in Jesus' teaching on asking, searching, and knocking (Matt 7:7–11; Luke 11:11–13), as among those worthy to receive a cup of water "in the name of a disciple" (Matt 10:42),[55] in a simile comparing "this generation" to children in the marketplaces (Matt 11:16–17; Luke 7:31–32), among the multitude of five thousand (Matt 14:21), of four thousand (Matt 15:38), as children sold into slavery in the parable of the Unforgiving Servant (Matt 18:25), and as children, "infants and nursing babies," who acclaimed Jesus at his triumphal entry into Jerusalem (Matt 21:15–16; see Ps 8:2).

Finally, in addition to the shared source material with Matthew and Mark above, Luke contains its own unrelated material. Because of this material and Luke's own birth narrative, children appear almost as significant in Luke as in Matthew's gospel. Non-adult children can be presumed in the following Lukan passages: in the infancy narratives of Jesus and John the Baptist (Luke 1:5–2:21), in the presentation of the boy Jesus at the temple and corresponding prophecies (Luke 2:22–38), in a teaching about prayer (Luke 11:7), as worthy of saving from danger on the Sabbath (Luke 14:3–5), as victims of Jerusalem's looming fate (Luke 19:44), and finally, in Jesus' lament of the foreseen destruction and desolation of Jerusalem on the way to his execution (Luke 23:28–29).

Obviously, when one reads these texts searching for children, they are not hard to find. I have provided this brief survey to show that, collectively, children play a critical role in each author's depiction of Jesus and his eschatological gathering, from insignificant appearances to pivotal roles.

Conceptions of Childhood: Now and Then

Turning to the historical study of children and childhood, Philippe Ariès is widely recognized as the initiator of this modern genre.[56] He firmly established that the concept of childhood had a history and could be studied. However, grounding his method on an examination of European sculptures, reliefs on tombstones, paintings, diaries and autobiographies, he argued that childhood, as a period in which children were treated distinctly from adults, was only discovered in the thirteenth century. Prior to

---

55. A distinct usage of Matthew in this context, it is particularly arguable whom the author intends "little ones" to refer to here, children or adult disciples. I include it here because some scholars take it to refer to children. Yet, as with the other occurrences, I shall evaluate these arguments in chapter 4.

56. Ariès, *Centuries of Childhood.*

this, Ariès noted that children were depicted in painting and relief as little adults, distinctive only in their size, not their features or dress. But since the thirteenth century, children have been increasingly depicted in distinctive dress, playing games adults no longer played, and sheltered from sexual awareness. Medieval Europeans understood that children were different from adults, but their society left little room for considering childhood as a developmental stage with its own needs and concerns. For Ariès, the seventeenth century represented the pivotal period for the emergence of childhood as a distinctive phase of development. Until the late sixteenth and early seventeenth centuries, parents tended to be rather unaffectionate and indifferent toward children, due largely to high infant mortality rates.[57] He attributed the change to a "revival" at this time in an interest in education by religious reformers seeking to instill greater morals into society. As a result, education became more prominent among middle class families, and parental affection and sentimentality correspondingly increased by the mid-eighteenth century.[58]

Similar to Ariès, yet methodologically different, Lloyd de Mause edited a pioneering anthology, *The History of Childhood*, just a few years later.[59] Covering history from late Roman antiquity to the present, de Mause has also been credited by scholars with helping to initiate the academic foray into childhood studies within the humanities. In his introductory essay, de Mause argues from an evolutionary historical perspective, asserting that humanity has only recently matured enough to value children as children.

> The history of childhood is a nightmare from which we have only recently begun to awaken. The further back in history one goes, the lower the level of child care, and the more likely children are to be killed, abandoned, beaten, terrorized, and sexually abused.[60]

To be fair, some of the scholars represented provide useful information, and for each period, themes such as birth, swaddling, wet-nursing and breast-feeding, discipline, apprenticing or otherwise placing children under the tutelage of others, and sexuality are examined. However, this work

57. Ibid., 38–39.

58. Ibid., 370. In a stark rebuke to Ariès, Pollock argued, over twenty years later, for a basic continuity of notions of childhood and awareness of children by parents between 1500 and 1900. Pollock, *Forgotten Children*.

59. de Mause, *History of Childhood*.

60. Ibid., 1.

was roundly criticized. The reliance to varying degrees on psycho-analytic methods limited this volume's usefulness.

The fundamental flaw of these early studies was their failure to push back further into the historical record, to seek out sources from classical antiquity. For a number of decades now, family and kinship studies have been a research niche among classical historians. By the 1980s and '90s, however, some Greco-Roman historians began to turn a lens specifically upon children and childhood. The fruit of their labors has decisively challenged notions that "childhood" is a modern discovery, or that parents had showed little affection for children before the seventeenth century. Instead, classical scholars such as Beryl Rawson, Suzanne Dixon, Mark Golden, and several others have shown that among the complexities of family life in ancient times, which certainly had its share of children that were abandoned, abused, or killed, there are a number of references to, and depictions or descriptions of, children that are quite sentimental or affectionate.[61] These will be fully examined in chapter two. For the moment, it is important to recognize that "childhood" as a developmental process was recognized long before Ariès suggested.

According to the Hellenized first-century Jew, Philo of Alexandria, Hippocrates distinguished stages of development in terms of the numerological importance of the number seven: παιδίου, παιδός, μειραχίου, νεανίσχου, ἀνδρός, πρεσβύτου, and γέροντος (*Opif.* 105). In the same context he attributes a sevenfold distinction of age development to Solon, the Athenian leader.

> While immature, a child, still an infant, grows his first set of teeth to last seven years. When God has completed another seven years, a sign of youthful maturing appears. As in a third, his limbs strengthen, his chin shows down; his changing complexion emerges. (*Opif.* 104)

The most methodical demarcation of childhood stages (for males) among Greco-Roman writers, by the Hellenistic librarian of Alexandria, Aristophanes of Byzantium, is transliterated by Mark Golden:

> *brephos*, the newborn; *paidion*, the nursling; *paidarion*, the child who can walk and speak; *paidiskos*; *pais*, roughly, the child who can be educated; *pallēks* or *boupais* or *antipais* or *mellephēbos*;

---

61. For example, see Dixon, *Roman Family*; *Childhood*; Golden, *Children and Childhood*; Rawson, *Family*; Rawson, *Marriage*; Wiedemann, *Adults and Children*.

ephēbos (and its local equivalents); *meirakion*; *meiraks*; *neaniskos*; *neanias*; and so on until old age.[62]

In addition to literary references, a number of images from Greek antiquity suggest some notion of childhood or development as distinct from adults. For example, the spring festival called the Anthesteria, in part, celebrated children, especially during the second day, Choes. Little wine juglets called *choes* were apparently given as gifts to children during this festival. The archaeological record suggests that as children grew, *choes* were made larger and were decorated with levels of "age appropriate activities." One depicts a baby crawling; another, a girl chasing a bird; still another depicts a young boy driving a chariot pulled by goats.[63]

Philo provides the clearest outline of stages in the life of a child among Jewish sources near the first century. In *De cherubim*, he uses the following sequence: infant, child, boy, youth, and young man (114). In *Quis rerum divinarum heres sit*, he speaks of the ages of infancy (to age seven) and of youth (presumably to age fourteen).

In addition to these literary references, various rituals among Greeks, Romans, and Jews recognized milestones in children's lives. Birth rituals are common. For Jews, the Abrahamic narratives attest to the importance of naming ceremonies and the advent of circumcision (Gen 17:1–5, 10–13), and Torah dictated boys were to be circumcised on the eighth day (Gen 17:10; Lev 12:3).[64] Among Greeks, one of the birth ceremonies, the *amphidromia*, consisted of gift-giving, a procession around the household hearth in which the father held the infant, a sacrifice, and the placement of a symbol above the door indicating a male or female birth. A livelier, more public celebration occurred on the tenth day, the *dekatē*, which involved dancing and the partaking of cake.[65] The Roman father's act of lifting up the child (*tollere*) symbolized his willingness to raise it. A purification ceremony, the

---

62. Golden includes a detailed discussion of the inconsistencies among the ancient sources on assigning particular age ranges to specific terms (Golden, *Children and Childhood*, 14–15). See also Golden, "Childhood," 15.

63. Korbin, "Prologue," 9. Also Golden, *Children and Childhood*, 42–43. For illustrations of some of these *choes*, see Neils, "Children and Greek Religion," 139–61, esp. 145–47. The catalogue of plates (195–312) contains amazing depictions of children of various ages engaged in various activities.

64. Cooper, *Child*, 14–15; Baumgarten, "Judaism," 43–45.

65. Golden, *Children and Childhood*, 23–24.

lustratio, took place on a Roman boy's ninth day (a girl's eighth day), and the child was named.[66]

Maturation and its attendant rituals and ceremonies could also mark an important milestone of development. Although entirely speculative, Luke's depiction of twelve-year-old Jesus learning from the teachers in the temple (2:41–52) might foreshadow the formal initiation of schooling attested by the Medieval period. Otherwise, a formal Jewish ritual associated with the onset of puberty is unattested in the biblical period.[67] Athenian children were introduced to their *phratries* as early as a year old and perhaps as late as seven at the Apaturia festival each fall. Boys experienced a coming of age festival associated with *hēbē*, the onset of puberty, although the sources and the complexity surrounding the term and its connotations have led to much disagreement among scholars regarding the age.[68] Athenian girls, perhaps only those of noble birth, may have spent a year playing the "little bear" (ἀρκτεία) at the sanctuary of Artemis at Brauron just before puberty, although Richard Hamilton convincingly argues the evidence regarding the ages and activities of the participants is very inconsistent.[69] In Roman society, boys wore the *bulla*, a pendant placed around their neck during the *lustratio* to ward off evil spirits, until they celebrated the maturation festival, the *toga uirilis*, and donned the toga signifying manhood.[70]

From the above survey, we can conclude that childhood and notions of development toward adulthood were certainly recognized by the societies important for this project. Once one reaches back beyond European medieval society to the Classical and Hellenistic Mediterranean, Ariès' thesis decisively fails. Childhood as a distinct period of development is firmly established, albeit culturally defined.

---

66. Rawson, "Adult-Child Relationships," 14–15.

67. Cooper, *Child*, 25–26; for sources on the later development of childhood rituals among Jews, see Baumgarten, "Judaism," 48–51.

68. Golden, *Children and Childhood*, 26–28.

69. Hamilton provides a critical evaluation of the problems presented by archaeological remains and literary sources, for example, Aristophanes, *Lysistrata* 641–47, in Hamilton, "Alkman," 449–72. See also Golden, *Children and Childhood*, 46–48, 76–79.

70. Rawson, "Adult-Child Relationships," 14.

Children in Gospels Studies

Childhood studies is an emerging field for biblical scholarship. From the advent of modern biblical scholarship in the 1800s through the 1970s, there remained a dearth of research focusing on children in the Bible, much less the Gospels.[71] In 1845, James Martineau argued against using much of the Bible in religious education. In his view, too many stories "contain the ideas, the passions, the moral sentiments, of a simple but savage people," and contain "constant bloodshed," among other material objectionable for the moral instruction of children.[72] Clearly education was Martineau's chief concern. Sunday-School was emerging in his day and such concerns, despite his colonialist worldview, were bound to emerge. In 1949, N. N. Ronning's *Jesus and the Children* presented a storybook introduction to a Jesus who was very child-friendly. It was a popular confessional book, complemented by simple illustrations. One can easily imagine a parent using the work to introduce this child-friendly Jesus to their children. To provide some context, Ronning described the child's world before Jesus as follows: "The story of child-life in pagan countries at all times and everywhere constitutes one of the darkest chapters in the history of mankind."[73] With brief, lurid descriptions of Roman and Germanic barbarity, not unlike some current scholars, Ronning established a sharp contrast between the former and Jesus.

> It is against this dark pagan background that Jesus' attitude toward children—His love, His understanding, His sympathy and tenderness is strikingly revealed in all its beauty . . . The great changes which have taken place in the world in the treatment of children are directly due to the influence of Jesus Christ.[74]

Academically rigorous studies in this early period included an intertextual analysis between the Synoptics and Paul by Robert M. Grant, which looked at the relationship between childhood and its metaphorical application to spiritual immaturity.[75] Meanwhile, Matthew Black presented a perceptive exegetical study of Mark 10:13–16, and its broader literary

---

71. Works of this early period but not described include Goddard, "Jesus," 456–65; McCown, "Child Training"; and Leaney, "Jesus and the Symbol," 91–92.

72. Martineau, *Bible and the Child*, 12.

73. Ronning, *Jesus and the Children*, 10.

74. Ibid., 10–11.

75. Grant, "Children in Mark," 71–73.

context. Arguing in part for an Aramaic background to Mark, he suggested that behind the Greek forms διάκονος (servant; Mark 9:35) and παιδίον (child; Mark 9:36) likely lay a single Aramaic term for both, *talya*. Black concluded that the purpose of Mark's interpretation of this pericope was to teach *adults* that true greatness is best conveyed through humble service, represented by the child.[76] By the 1960s and '70s, a handful of articles and monographs explored theological implications of various texts for children within the Church, including issues of infant baptism, child evangelism, and the idea of sonship in the Pauline corpus.[77] The exception of this period was a 1969 monograph by Simon Légasse, *Jésus et l'enfant*. In this study Légasse examines whether children or childhood constituted a coherent theme in the Synoptic Gospels. Similar to this book, he considered the relationship between children and Jesus as well as children and the Synoptic authors. However, he was more interested in historical questions, which necessitated a form-critical approach. What was the relationship between Jesus and children? How were they theologically important for him? How did these passages on children function for the early Church? Légasse focused primarily on teachings where children are seemingly centered and largely ignored miracle stories. He argued that the children reflected in the Synoptic Gospels were used to illustrate some point about the paucity of a desired behavior, such as complete dependence on God, in the adult disciples of Jesus.

In the 1980s, a number of exegetical studies were published. A handful of essays were the product of the "Third Quest" by Jesus researchers, who published exegetical studies of gospel sayings related to children and the kingdom. For example, the essays by Vernon K. Robbins and John Dominic Crossan were concerned with form-critical analyses using the form of the *chreia* as their comparative model. Daniel Patte utilized a structural analysis of these passages to show their semantic and organizational differences. Although they present significant exegetical studies on the most important gospel passages about children and the kingdom, these essays, and their

---

76. Black, "Markan Parable," 14–16.

77. In rough chronological order we find the following: Schilling, "What Means the Saying," 56–58; Beasley-Murray, "Church and Child," 206–18; Clements, "Relation of Children," 195–205; Lockyer, *All the Children*; Pridmore, *Theology of Childhood*; Shelley, "An Exegetical Study"; Boadt, "Child in the Bible," 2082–88; Weber, "Gospel in the Child," 227–33; and Weber, *Jesus and the Children*.

reviewers, were actually concerned with issues other than children as a field of study.[78]

In a similar vein, an article by Jerome Kodell and a chapter by Ernest Best in his book *Disciples and Discipleship* (1986) provide excellent exegetical studies of passages concerned with Jesus and children, but they were not wholly concerned with children per se. Best's examination of Mark 10:13–16 is significant for our discussion and will be drawn upon in chapter three. First, Best examined the importance of this pericope "for Mark and the community to which he was writing," rather than for what it tells us about Jesus.[79] Second, through a detailed form and redactional exegesis of the passage, Best argued Mark's addition of vv.14c and 15 to pre-Markan material make the pericope explicitly about discipleship.[80] Therefore, Mark's concern is instruction about discipleship to *adult followers*, not a discourse on the importance of children to Jesus.

> For Mark, attention is not being directed to the need to *bring children* but to the requirement to be *like children* in receiving the Kingdom. This is appropriate to the main drive of the Gospel at this point, namely discipleship . . . Thus if the original pericope depicted Jesus' attitude to children, this has almost disappeared through the additions made to it and the context with which it has been provided.[81]

In a manner similar to Best, Kodell examines Luke 9:46–56 and 18:9–23, bookends to Luke's "great interpolation," which assess Luke's arrangement and redaction of the Markan pericopae on children. His exegesis and contextualization of the two principal units on children demonstrate clearly how Luke reshaped these pericopae in order to buttress the themes of lowliness and receptivity, Luke's vision of discipleship. As a result, Luke is more concerned about the character of *childlikeness* for would-be followers than about the actual relationship between children and the kingdom. Likewise,

---

78. Upon the suggestion of John D. Crossan, the discussion within the entire issue of *Semeia* 29 is thematically arranged around gospels passages involving children and the kingdom. Patte, "Jesus Pronouncement," 3–42; Robbins, "Pronouncement Stories," 43–74; Crossan, "Kingdom and Children," 75–96.

79. Best, *Disciples*, 80.

80. The "Markan additions" to 10:13–16 according to Best are: "[F]or it is to such as these that the kingdom of God belongs. Truly I tell you, whoever does not receive the kingdom of God as a little child will never enter it" (Best, *Disciples*, 94).

81. Best, *Disciples*, 94; my emphasis.

Kodell is more concerned about Luke's compositional choices than about the plight of children in the text.[82]

There are, however, a few works in the 1980s that began to think more critically about children in the text, even if their principal focus was on Jesus. For example, in 1983, J. Duncan M. Derrett published an exegetical study of Mark 10:13–16 that would later become a foundation piece of Judith Gundry-Volf's portrait of the child-friendly Jesus.[83] The thrust of Derrett's argument is that, by embracing (ἐναγκαλισάμενος; 9:36 and 10:16) the children brought to him, Jesus enacted a symbolic adoption of these children. Therefore, they became co-heirs to his kingdom. The blessing (and adoption) of Ephraim and Manasseh by Jacob in Genesis 48 is presented as analogous to Mark's "blessing," a connection known by seventeenth and eighteenth century interpreters, but lost among nineteenth- and twentieth-century commentators. In an interesting weave of scripture and prophetical interpretation, Derrett argues that the blessings (read *adoption*) of Ephraim and Manasseh directly bear on the messianic expectation, and Jesus' concern for children. Since Derrett's article has provided the underpinning for the more recent work of Gundry-Volf, who in turn has become foundational for several current inquiries on Jesus and children, his argument will play an important role in chapters three and four of this study.

Three more examples from the 1980s placed children at the center of biblical inquiry. One came from the African Episcopal scholar Anthony O. Nkwoka; another from Catholic scholar Guy Bedouelle; the final one from Paulette Taylor-Wingender. Nkwoka provided an insightful analysis of Mark 10:13–16, ultimately in order to pose thoughtful challenges to the treatment of children in the modern church. Meanwhile, his exegesis of the pericope presented a pattern that has become familiar in studies of Jesus, the gospels, and children: Jesus is presented as *unique* in the treatment of children among his contemporaries.

> The way, the manner, and the circumstances under which Jesus received and blessed the children, which finds no parallel in ancient literature as a whole, lays an irresistible incumbency on the Church. Jesus was very busy in the last few months before His death, yet He found time for children. The scribes had no time for children, let alone a rabbi like Jesus.[84]

82. Kodell, "Luke and the Children," 415–30.

83. Derrett, "Why Jesus Blessed," 1–18.

84. Nkwoka, "Mark 10:13–16," 104.

More than Nkwoka, Bedouelle was principally concerned with legitimating infant baptism and a greater participation of children in the modern Catholic Church.[85] Meanwhile, Taylor-Wingender fashioned a convincing argument from Matthew against modern practices of child evangelism. Foundational to her position was a particularly astute analysis of Matthew 18:1–5 and its context, where she argued that children *already* possess the kingdom (19:14). They do not need conversion, the adults do; and to do so they must become like children, vulnerable and humble.[86]

However, probably in part due to the emergence of childhood studies among scholars of classical and Greco-Roman antiquity in the 1980s, biblical and theological scholarship on children *as children* finally began to take off in the 1990s. Because of the sharp rise in the number of essays whose chief concern becomes children in the Bible at this time, I shall only highlight those that center on the Synoptic Gospels, or that may serve an important function for the present study. Some of the better contributors to the field in the 1990s include Stephen C. Barton, Peter Müller, and William A. Strange.[87]

In 1991, Stephen C. Barton published a chapter entitled "Jesus-Friend of Little Children?" in *The Contours of Christian Education*. In this brief chapter, Barton argues that children are (and *were*) very important as metaphors for the various configurations of discipleship portrayed by the gospel writers. Despite extreme brevity, his survey of each gospel is very instructive, foremost because he begins each gospel subsection by reviewing the evangelist's chief ethical theme (e.g., humility in Matthew).[88] From these sources, he posits three probable characteristics emblematic of the historical Jesus' relationship with children: 1) that children "have a share in the kingdom of God," 2) Jesus taught his followers that they must receive the kingdom "as a child," and 3) his followers' kindness and hospitality will be measured by their treatment of the most marginal, especially children. These characteristics, on the one hand, suggest Jesus was a "friend of little

85. Bedouelle, "Reflection," 349–67.

86. Taylor-Wingender, "Kids of the Kingdom," 18–25.

87. It should be noted that, at this time, Crossan adds significantly, once again, to the interpretation of Mark 9:36–37 and 10:13–16 (and their corresponding parallels), first through his monumental work *Historical Jesus*, esp. 266–69, and subsequently in the more popular abbreviated form, *Jesus*, esp. 62–64. Yet Crossan remains very much interested in what these passages tell us about Jesus and/or the kingdom, not what they tell us about children for their own sake.

88. Barton, "Jesus-Friend," 35–40.

children." On the other hand, Barton carefully shows that their significance for Jesus lay chiefly in their pedagogical function as a metaphor for adult discipleship.[89]

Two other points about the essay are noteworthy. First, among the limitations Barton lists for studying children in the gospels are the facts that 1) the disciples were asked to subordinate their family obligations to Jesus, and 2) there is no indication Jesus ever directed his teachings to children. Second, Barton raises such provoking critiques of our foray into the study of Jesus' relationship to children that they are worth quoting at length.

> It is possible that the psychological, social and institutional invest-
> ment in children so characteristics of modernity may lead us to
> see in the gospels little more than the reflection of our own needs
> and to interpret them only in ways which justify our prior invest-
> ment. To what extent, for example, is the Jesus who is the friend
> of little children a coded way of idealizing *children* (by associating
> them with Jesus), the consequence of which is, by so distancing
> ourselves from children, to avoid acting responsibly toward them
> as actual human beings? Or is it a way of idealizing *Jesus* (by as-
> sociating him with "little children") in order to keep at a distance
> the claims that he makes upon our lives as adults? Alternatively,
> does the picture of Jesus as the children's friend express a desire to
> find in Jesus the friend of the child *in us*? Such possibilities are no
> less real for being hidden.

Although I disagree with Barton's acceptance of Ariès' thesis, we must be cautious about permitting our "western fascination with children and the sentimentalizing of childhood" (and I would add *of Jesus*) to derive theological conclusions which the texts might not support.[90] Alone, this small chapter raises some noteworthy issues for child studies, but Barton has developed a solid reputation in household and family studies of the New Testament. His work will be foundational to parts of this study.

In the same year, Peter Müller published the fruits of his *Habilita-tionsschrift* on passages related to children, *In der Mitte der Gemeinde: Kinder im Neuen Testament*. He argues that children were, in reality and metaphorically, *central* to early Christian communities.[91] Above all, Müller provides a detailed exegetical study of several New Testament passages on children. His exegesis of Mark 10:13–16 sets the tone; it is the only passage

89. Ibid., 33–34, 39.

90. Both points given, including the block quote, are from ibid., 32–33.

91. Müller, *In der Mitte*, 392.

that receives its own chapter. Methodologically, he begins with *Formge-schichte* then shifts to a detailed study of its *Sitz im Leben*, where he situates 10:13–16 in a discussion over the limitation of children within a Markan congregational setting.[92] Although his lack of reference to any of the recent Greco-Roman studies on children limits his work, his exegesis informs this study.

In 1996, a comprehensive monograph on children was published by William A. Strange, *Children in the Early Church*.[93] Strange's central concern is to understand why the early Church appears so silent about the presence and role of children, when Jesus seemed quite concerned about them. Entirely concerned with the presence of children, his first chapter provides a survey of Jewish, Greek, and Roman attitudes about children—within their family settings, and within the context of their societies. In chapter two, Strange examines the presence of children in the canonical Gospels. The thematically arranged subsections of chapter two are particularly helpful and include one on the birth accounts and childhood of Jesus, one on Jesus and children, one on the disciples and children, and one on parent-child relations. From there he goes on to examine their presence in the New Testament epistles and in the early centuries of the Church. A major component of his study is the relationship of children to the sacraments, infant baptism and children vis-à-vis the Eucharist, in the early Church.

While focusing on the Gospels, Strange does not shy from making definitive conclusions about Jesus' relationship with children. "[C]hildren did count for something in the ministry of Jesus . . . We find that Jesus was an observer of children . . . (Matt. 11:16–19). One of the distinctive features of Jesus' message and ministry was the significance he attributed to children."[94] Strange credits Jewish culture with conveying the importance of children to Jesus by emphasizing their education and legal protection from exposure at birth; they are viewed as a blessing, potential inheritors of God's covenant promises. Yet, Strange's interpretation of children in the Gospels serves to underscore the uniqueness of Jesus.

> The rabbis made provision for teaching children, and for their thorough initiation into the ways of their ancestors. Jesus' openness to

---

92. Ibid., 72–78.
93. Strange, *Children*.
94. Ibid., 38.

children was *for their own sake,* not principally for *their potential,*
and it was something unique to his ministry.[95]

Despite this enthusiasm for attention to children by Jesus (or is Jesus' uniqueness being foregrounded?), Strange concludes chapter two with
a sober assessment of "Jesus' attitude to children." On the one hand, he
declared the kingdom belonged to them too; he dealt with them similar
to other marginalized groups (women, tax collectors, etc.). On the other
hand, "he had no recorded ministry to children apart from their parents";
nor did he "call them to discipleship."[96] Above all, Strange's book serves
as one of the earliest *significant* contributions to the emergent interest in
children *as children* in New Testament scholarship.

This selection of works has been intentionally concise and focused.
There are several other brief or otherwise popular contributions from this
decade. Children are the central focus of many of these works as well. Their
once typical status as peripheral objects of narrative or investigation decidedly begins to recede amidst the growing tide of interest in childhood
studies. As we enter this millennium, children and childhood studies of
the Bible have only grown. Therefore, the final section of this survey will
likewise be limited to contributions deemed especially significant for this
particular study.

Perhaps as a symbol of how important children have become in modern society, *Theology Today* began the new millennium with an issue (56,
4) devoted entirely to the theme of children. The following year, *Interpretation* did likewise (55, 2); and in 2002, the *Jahrbuch fur biblische Theologie*
17 followed suit. Similarly, three anthologies have been recently published:
The Child in Christian Thought (2001),[97] *The Child in the Bible* (2008),[98]
and *The Child and Childhood in World Religions* (2009).[99] Each was edited
in part by Marcia Bunge and contains one or more chapters that cover the
Gospels. Finally, the Annual Meeting of the Society of Biblical Literature
inaugurated its first section on Children and the Bible in the fall of 2009.

Within these venues, names that have emerged, sometimes more than
once, with significant contributions to children in the Gospels and/or Jesus

95. Ibid., 50; my emphasis.

96. Ibid., 64.

97. Bunge, ed., *Child in Christian Thought.*

98. Bunge et al., *Child in the Bible.*

99. Browning and Bunge, eds., *Children and Childhood in World Religions.*

include: Judith M. Gundry-Volf,[100] John T. Carroll,[101] Keith J. White,[102] and Peter Müller.[103] Meanwhile, among the most significant contributions of the 2000s not directly related to these three venues is a monograph by Peter Balla.[104] Since the present work centers in the Synoptic Gospels, the essays by Gundry on Mark, Carroll on Luke, and White on Matthew are probably the most important for this study. After his *In der Mitte der Gemeinde*, Müller decidedly reads the children vis-à-vis Jesus as metaphorically important for adult disciples. Therefore, his latter essays are less useful for the exegetical component of this study. Balla's monograph deals largely with *adult-children* in relation to their parents, but his examination of the Gospels cannot be ignored. Furthermore, chapters two and three on Greek, Latin, and Jewish sources regarding child-parent relationships, from the Hellenistic period to roughly the third century CE, provide useful contextualization for the present study.

Aside from the monographs of Müller and Strange, probably no other New Testament scholar has been more influential in childhood studies than Judith Gundry. In a handful of articles and chapters from 2000 to 2008, Gundry has written explicitly about the place of children in the New Testament, especially the Gospels, and Mark in particular. Her overall thesis is that the marginal status of children is challenged by Jesus in the Gospels. The Synoptic authors place Jesus in relation to children: healing them, blessing them, and characterizing them as the quintessence of discipleship for the kingdom of God.

In an early article she focuses on Mark 9:36–37 (and par.) and 10:13–16 (and par.) where children become the vehicle for teaching about discipleship and the kingdom of God. From Mark 9, where Jesus receives a young child in the midst of the disciples, Gundry asserts that "to be great in the reign of God, disciples have to love and serve children." She further concludes:

---

100. In earlier publications, her name is given as Gundry-Volf, while simply given as Gundry in later articles. For simplicity, I shall henceforth refer to her by her most recent nomenclature. Gundry-Volf, "To Such as These," 469–80; Gundry-Volf, "Least and the Greatest," 29–60; and Gundry, "Children," 143–76.

101. Carroll, "Children in the Bible," 121–34; "What Then Will This Child Become?," 177–94.

102. White, "He Placed a Little Child," 353–74.

103. Müller, "Die Metapher"; and "Gottes Kinder," 141–62.

104. Balla, *Child-Parent Relationship*.

Jesus' teaching about receiving children as the mark of true greatness places children at the center of the community's attention as
prime objects of its love and service, and requires of all who would
be great in the community to serve children.[105]

Therefore, rejecting a child is tantamount to rejecting God. Meanwhile, in
chapter ten, Mark's Jesus has just finished teaching on marriage and divorce
when the author writes:

And they were bringing young children (παιδία) to him so that he
might touch them. But the disciples denounced them. But watch-
ing, Jesus became irate and said to them, "Let the young children
(τὰ παιδία) come to me; do not hold them back, for the kingdom
of God consists of such like these. Truly I tell you, whoever does
not welcome the kingdom of God like a young child (παιδίον) will
never enter it." And having taken them into his arms, he placed
his hands upon them and began blessing them. (Mark 10:13–16)

Gundry points out that v.14 stresses that "Children *qua children* . . . are the
intended recipients of the reign of God. It has come for them." Why does
Jesus speak of children in this manner? For Gundry, the answer lies in the
Beatitudes, where Jesus taught that the lowly and powerless are the primary
beneficiaries of the reign of God.[106] Finally, Gundry adopts the interpretation of Willi Egger in v.15, reading "as a child" to mean that adults must,
like Jewish children, enter the kingdom not through adherence to the Law,
but by simply complete and utter dependence on the mercy of God.[107] Gundry also spends time discussing the peculiar adaptations of Mark's material
in Matthew's parallels, but I shall combine this discussion with my review
of White.

Through her examination of these texts, Gundry sharply contrasts the
inclusiveness of children in the ministry of Jesus with the contemporary
cultural norms that relegated them to a marginal social status. Children are
not unimportant beings, readily exposed as unwanted infants. Nor are they
only important for their potential as adults. Rather, Jesus taught that children exemplified the best characteristics of discipleship. Her research has

105. Gundry, "To Such as These," 475–76.

106. Ibid., 472. With few changes, except the addition of a review of Hellenistic attitudes to children, and an examination of children in New Testament epistles, this article
was incorporated into the initial anthology on children and religion by Marcia Bunge:
Gundry, "The Least and the Greatest," 29–60.

107. Gundry, "To Such as These," 473–74.

been influential in recent theological works including Marin E. Marty,[108] Tom Thatcher,[109] and Bonnie J. Miller-McLemore.[110]

Gundry focuses more narrowly on Mark's depictions of children in 2008. I have reviewed this essay for the online *Journal of Childhood and Religion*,[111] and Bonnie Miller-McLemore shares some of my criticisms of Gundry's work.[112] In this essay, Gundry reiterates that children also are given "full and equal participation in the eschatological reign of God,"[113] and they are models for how one enters this reign.[114] New to her analysis is her incorporation of J. Duncan M. Derrett's thesis that Jesus' embrace and blessing in 10:13–16 represents an adoption (cf. Gen 48), by which Jesus' assumes a "parental role" in order to bless them before his death.

I have identified three problems with Gundry's work in my review. First, consciously or not, her reading privileges Jesus as extraordinarily unique for his time. In a footnote in her 2000 article, she intimates there might be problems with her construction, in light of sayings that leave Jesus "seemingly inimical . . . toward children."[115] But more recently, she asserts that Jesus' actions and teaching actually revitalized the family, through healing sick children, exorcizing demons from them, or raising them from the dead.[116] Suggestions of estrangement or detachment raised by the Jesus movement in the Synoptic Gospels are played down (e.g., Mark 1:16–20; 3:20–21, 31–35; 6:1–6a; 13:9–13 and par.).[117] Second, she claims that by becoming a follower of Jesus, one "explicitly does not" replace a follower's "family of origin" with a new fictive kinship. Rather one's family simply becomes extended to encompass the community of disciples.[118] Yet, in my opinion, she does not fully treat the implications of discipleship by those

---

108. Marty, *Mystery of the Child*.

109. Thatcher, "Beginning Again," 2010.

110. Miller-McLemore, *Let the Children Come*.

111. Murphy, Review of *Child in the Bible*, 5–7.

112. Miller-McLemore, "Jesus Loves the Little Children," 1–35.

113. Gundry, "Children," 143.

114. Ibid., 146.

115. Gundry, "To Such as These," 471n1.

116. Gundry, "Children," 160, 162.

117. Miller-McLemore also just recognized this problem, "Jesus Loves the Little Children," 11–14, 17.

118. Gundry, "Children," 159–60. Also see Miller-McLemore, "Jesus and the Little Children," 17–18.

who chose to leave everything to follow Jesus. Third, while Gundry asserts the near uniqueness of Jesus' expressions toward children, she simultaneously downplays evidence of affection, sentimentality, and concern for children in the Hellenistic world of Jesus' day.[119]

Problem & Restatement of Thesis

This leads me to state the problem as I see it. I agree that the Synoptic authors challenge the marginalization of children. For instance, Mark emphasizes the *dependent* quality of children, and expects adult disciples to emulate this quality.[120] Luke depicts a reversal of social norms and radical inclusiveness of the marginalized in the kingdom of God, including children.[121] Challenging their marginal status is *one* way to interpret these texts. With respect to children, had the Synoptic authors concluded their accounts of Jesus' eschatological gathering with the "blessing of the children," then the narrative foregrounding of children as worthy of hospitality (Mark 9:37 and par.) and emulation (Mark 10:15 and par.) would seem unparalleled. Yet, the narratives continue; children appear less; Jesus and the disciples move on. As a result, the Synoptic authors' depictions cannot fully obscure the special challenges for non-adult children presented by respective characterizations of Jesus' activity. In addition, scholars have not examined the inclusion of children against sayings relativizing family ties and the lifestyle indicative of the radical call to discipleship of the broader Synoptic narratives. This study fills this lacuna in the field by arguing that the Synoptic authors *rhetorically* raise the social presence of children in their narratives to an unprecedented level, but cannot mitigate the natural

119. On this point I included a footnote in my review that states: "Gundry recognizes this sentimentality (158) and footnotes most of these sources. Still, it is puzzling to me why she does not present some of their more sentimental findings regarding children," (Murphy, Review of *Child in the Bible*, 6n1; for the entirety of my critique, see pages 6–9). This is specifically in reference to her 2008 essay on Mark. She gave a much more extensive treatment of Hellenistic source material in 2001, referencing some negative *and positive* assessments of children and childhood from Greek and Roman sources. Yet she dwells at length on the exposure and infanticide of infants in these cultures without delving into the complexity of rationales behind such practices. The result of juxtaposing this characterization of a few "pagan" practices with Jesus' embrace of children, as I have suggested, "merely serves as a straw man that further constructs the uniqueness of Jesus," (Murphy, Review of *Child in the Bible*, 6).

120. Gundry, "Children," 169–70.

121. Carroll, "What Then Will This Child Become?," 178, 188–89.

challenges of childhood in relation to the demands placed on disciples in the kingdom. In short, rather than the concern and affection of Jesus for children, the Synoptic authors present child characters with challenges of household disruption and alienation as a consequence of the in-breaking of the kingdom of God.

Outline of Study

First, I begin in chapter two with a socio-historical analysis of children in Second-Temple Judaism and Hellenistic-Roman antiquity in order to understand the social parameters under which our first-century authors finalized their stories.[122] Were children welcomed and treated as objects of affection by Jewish, Greek, and Roman adults around the first century? To what degree are the gospels' attentions to children unique in antiquity? Are there examples of children depicted as autonomous beings, exhibiting agency independent of caregivers?

Chapter 3 consists of an examination of passages centering on a child or children to explore how the Synoptic authors *attempt to convince us* of the relationship between children, the kingdom, and discipleship. Particular attention is given to passages where the Synoptic authors emphasize a concern for children by Jesus. This includes the depictions of Jesus healing children (Mark 5:22–24, 35–43 and par.; Mark 7:25–30/Matt 15:21–28; Mark 9:17–29 and par.), the narrative foregrounding of a child as an exemplary member of the kingdom of God (Mark 9:33–37 and par.), as well as a story of caregivers bringing children to Jesus for him to bless (Mark 10:13–16 and par.).

Chapter 4 consists of a close deconstructive reading of the same passages from chapter three, this time attending to the ambiguous nature of key terms and phrases and incompatibilities imbedded in the narratives, while also juxtaposing these passages with passages or themes that problematize the theme of inclusiveness toward children by the Synoptic authors. This will bring into sharper focus: Jesus' sayings that relativize family ties (e.g., Mark 3:31–35; Luke 14:26 and parallels, as well as others); Jesus' lifestyle clearly characterized in the Synoptics as itinerant (Mark 6:7–11 and par.); and elements of the passion where a theme of abandonment can

122. To stay relatively contemporary with the time period of the Gospels and avoid unnecessarily broadening this study, I shall limit my investigation to the period of approximately 300 BCE to 200 CE.

be interpreted in Jesus' willful separation from his newly created kingdom family. This chapter shows how the Synoptic Gospels deconstruct themselves, raising questions such as: How would a child be affected if he or she could accept the call to discipleship by Jesus in these gospels? What would the impact be on this child if one or both parents were to accept such a summons? What does child-inclusion mean in texts that expect many families to socially implode, where a leader and followers that are constantly on the move, and whose passion sustains a theme of abandonment at several levels? As with feminist/womanist interpretation, this child-centered reading will bring a "hermeneutic of suspicion" to the text, scrutinizing how children are portrayed. Are they celebrated or exploited, protected or abandoned by adult characters in the Synoptic accounts? At the very least, this interpretive reading should arouse caution when reading for children in the Gospels, and cause us to reflect one more time on how seriously we do or do not bring the day-to-day demands of children to our reading of the Bible.

Chapter 5 is a theological reflection on the issues raised by this study. I begin with some statistics on modern day child abuse and neglect, followed by some theological questions to ponder. Then, I attempt my own imaginative literary [re]construction of a few encounters of children and Jesus in the gospels. I end by challenging readers to reconsider seriously not only the promises and positive visions of children in the Bible, but to embrace its conundrums and allow room for viable, even if less desirable, interpretations by readers who bring diverse experiences to these texts.

CHAPTER TWO

OUT OF THE SHADOWS

> [W]ithout anyone having preached or called for it . . ., many thou-
> sands of boys, ranging in age from six years to full maturity, left
> the plows or carts which they were driving, the flocks which they
> were pasturing, and anything else which they were doing. This
> they did despite the wishes of their parents, relatives, and friends
> who sought to make them draw back. Suddenly one ran after an-
> other to take the cross. Thus, by groups of twenty, or fifty, or a
> hundred, they put up banners and began to journey to Jerusalem
> . . . whether they crossed to the Holy Land or what their end was is
> uncertain. One thing is sure: that of the many thousands who rose
> up, only very few returned.[1]

THE QUOTATION ABOVE, CHRONICLED from Cologne, is one of the few
fragments which suggests that waves of non-adult children were able to
suddenly leave their household relations and duties for some form of a divine call to "liberate" the Holy Sepulcher in Jerusalem from the Saracens.
Although recorded over a thousand years after the Gospels, it does not
fail to capture the essentially agrarian life of those who "accepted the call,"
a lifestyle not entirely unlike a large portion of the advanced agrarian
empire of early imperial Rome and its provinces. Its author would have us
believe that children could easily leave their households and willingly give

---

1. This is one of the few sources on the so-called "Children's Crusade" of 1212
(Brundage, *Crusades*, 213). In a recent critique of the standard characterization of these
movements, Peter Raedts argues from social and linguistic analysis that most of these
crusaders should be understood as poor people, not children. Rather, it was the accounts
from the following or third generation removed that embellished the "child" aspect of
these movements. See Raedts, "Children's Crusade," 279–324.

their lives over to God's purposes. Some recent biblical scholars who have brought children to the foreground in the Synoptics have understood them to be situated within Jesus' new fictive family or realm,[2] occasionally even blurring the distinction between narrative and actual history. For example, although Keith White sets out to take "a narrative approach to the text," perhaps wishful thinking leads him to state that "there is good reason to suppose that [children] eagerly followed [Jesus], listened to his stories, and rejoiced in the signs that he did."[3]

Because of such shifts in thinking from purported narrative approaches to questions of history, it is necessary to examine what our Synoptic authors might have reasonably understood about children in and around the first century. Furthermore, it is asserted by some scholars that, unlike the surrounding world, the Synoptic authors and Jesus were concerned about children as children, not for what they might become. In response to such assertions, questions about children specific to this study are brought to our sources. The guiding question at hand is: Could children have engaged as agents, e.g., embarked upon a lifestyle of discipleship? Or, how plausible are the Synoptic authors' depictions of children as "kingdom" adherents—could children have fulfilled such a role? In other words, what could children actually do *as children* that the readers of the Synoptic Gospels would think plausible? Within the parameters of this question, there are a range of sub-questions that must be answered. Do our sources suggest parents and children were sentimental or affectionate toward each other? Supposing we envision children as followers of Jesus, what were the socially determined practices for raising children? In order to answer these and other questions about children in the ancient world, we must examine Jewish and Hellenistic-Roman sources. Unless necessitated by one of these questions, the basic growth, education, and maturation of children in antiquity have been adequately described by other scholars and will not be repeated here.

However, a word of caution is in order. The Hellenistic-Roman world between the third centuries BCE and CE was a geographically expansive area with many sub regions, a mixture of urban and rural populations, and diverse traditions. Simply stated, the Hellenistic-Roman world was

---

2. For Gundry, Mark defines such followers as those who *do* the will of God (Gundry, "Children," 158). For Carroll, Luke situates children as "honored guests" in the ministry of Jesus (Carroll, "What Then Will This Child Become?," 178), yet he is careful to note the *potentially* subversive nature of this ministry to traditional families (ibid., 185–87).

3. White, "He Placed a Little Child," 356 and 362 respectively.

complex. Although a bit early for this study, the great differences in Greek family structure between Athens and Sparta attest to the problems inherent in characterizing the world of children. Likewise, there must have been some complexity and diversity between Jewish families of antiquity. At the least I can imagine families in the Diaspora, Hellenistic-Jewish families, Essene families, and Pharisaic families. The point is that it goes without saying how problematic it might be to view Jewish, Greek, or Roman childhood monolithically. Still, it is necessary to come to some tentative generalizations about childhood for background to the Synoptic authors. Furthermore, some of our evidence is prescriptive, especially sources for Jewish childhood, while some is descriptive.

Jewish, Greek, and Latin Sources

Our evidence on children among Jews, including Jewish children, slave children, and others, roughly between 300 BCE-200 CE is scattered among literary sources such as Philo, Josephus, the intertestamental works, the Pseudepigrapha, the Dead Sea Scrolls, and the four Gospels. Unlike other studies that treat the Gospels separately from Jewish sources, I propose that, with care, these sources ought to be treated as sources for childhood and family life in Judaism.[4] First, it is seldom clear that children and their caregivers portrayed in the Gospels have turned from one form of Judaism to become followers of Jesus, despite their function to emphasize the in-breaking of the kingdom of God. Unfortunately, because of the Jewish prohibition on images, we have no images of children or domesticity from the ancient Jewish world to aid our investigation.

Meanwhile, our evidence on children in the Hellenistic-Roman world roughly between 300 BCE-200 CE seems vast in comparison to Jewish source material. Works entirely consumed with children or adult-child relations include Plutarch, *De Amore Prolis* (in *Moralia* VI), where he argues, contra Epicurus, that humans have a natural affection for children, and that children are not simply raised for one's material support in old age. He also wrote a work entitled *The Education of Children* (in *Moralia* I), and the Latin writer Quintilian weighs and discusses pedagogical techniques in *Institutio oratoria* and expresses great emotion over the death of his son. Some of Cicero's works, particularly his *Epistulae ad Atticum*, contain passages expressing a good deal of sentiment and concern over children

4. See Eisenbaum, *Paul.*

amidst his own household, broadly speaking, which bears on the domestic and public spheres of Roman life. In addition to these texts, there are a number of more succinct references to children across a wide spectrum of Hellenistic and Roman sources, as well as epigraphic and artistic sources bearing on children, which will be cited where appropriate.

Children in the Jewish World

First, some basic ontological assumptions are usually made concerning Jewish views of children, filtered down from Hebrew traditions predating Hellenism. For instance, the family was instituted from the beginning, through the creation and fall of humanity. Male and female were said to be creations of God and were told to have offspring (Gen 1:26–28). As a result of this belief, accounts of unmarried adult men are exceptional in the Hebrew Bible. Marriage and raising children appear to be strong normative elements of Jewish tradition.

Given Genesis' situation of children within God's creative act, theologians often assume or assert that Jews held *all children* in greater esteem than their contemporaries. The point is certainly arguable, and might depend upon whether "Jews" collectively or distinctly refers to the Jewish people, Jewish tradition, and/or the god of Israel. In a recent contribution to the biblical study of children, Walter Brueggemann has argued that the Hebrew Bible portrays Israel's god as decidedly concerned about the welfare and justice of all children, typified by passages relating to the care of orphans (Deut 10:17–18; Hosea 14:3; Ps 10:14, 17–18; 68:5; 146:9). But as I have argued elsewhere, more often Jewish tradition, at least in parts of the Hebrew Bible, does not share the same concern for children other than its own.[5] It seems more precise to say that (homogenously speaking for the moment) Jewish tradition greatly esteemed its own children, brought into a covenant relationship with Israel's god. Even the "image of God"

---

5. That is, Israelite children and what he calls "other children" (Brueggemann, "Vulnerable Children," 399–422). Cf. Jensen, *Graced Vulnerability*, 3. I believe that Brueggemann's use of the term "other" is misplaced. If "other" means "outsiders," children not among the covenant people, then we should be talking about Canaanite children, Philistine children, Egyptian children, the unmentioned children of the flood generation, and the like (Murphy, Review of *Child in the Bible*, 8–9). When considered together, the texts presented by Jensen (Exodus and Leviticus) and Brueggemann (Deuteronomy) demonstrate the cleavage in Jewish tradition over the "alien" within. The former books exhort Israelites not to oppress them; the latter commands their destruction.

implication of Genesis 1:26–27 is inconsistently applied to descendants of Abraham in the remainder of that book.[6] Rather than a holistic view, it is probably better to argue instead for a diversity of Jewish thought about families and children by the centuries important to this study.

What did children mean to or for Jewish parents and caregivers in the period of our study? Is there evidence they were valued as children, or merely for the roles they would assume as adults? Is there evidence of affection or sentimentality for children? How rooted in and dependent on their families were children in the Jewish world, and is there evidence to suggest children acted autonomously to become learners in prophetic circles or of philosophic or religious schools?

Christian theologians frequently point out that ancient Jews refrained from birth control[7] and abhorred practices that would limit family growth, such as abortion, infanticide, or exposure.[8] Since the present work is concerned only with the presence of post-natal children, I shall limit my argument here to discussions of infanticide and exposure, and will reserve discussions of Jewish contraception and abortion for a later date. The reason generally given by theologians is that life was more valued in Jewish tradition; like their progenitors, children are made in the "image of God."[9] As Marianne Thompson writes: "Created by God, and protected by the law of God, the child derives her identity and status from the God who created her, and this affords the child unique protection."[10] Furthermore, couples are told to "multiply" and fill the earth (Gen 1:28).

Despite such prescriptive assertions about the positive place of children, children faced terrible threats in the ancient Jewish world. In addition to natural universally occurring threats such as illness or deformity,

6. For example, see Fretheim, "God Was with the Boy," 3–23, and again, see Murphy, Review of *Child in the Bible*, 3–4.

7. But see Safrai, "Home and Family," 764, where types of birth control are discussed, including cloth or wool tampons and withdrawal of the penis before ejaculation. Also, see Millen, *Women*, 21–54, who decisively shows that birth control was accepted within the framework of early Judaism.

8. Gundry, "Children," 162; Strange, *Children*, 4; Bakke, *When Children Became People*, 110–14.

9. Towner, "Children in the Image of God," 307–23; Thompson, "Children in the Gospel of John," 204–05; Fretheim, "God Was with the Boy," 4; Horn and Martens, *Let the Little Children Come*, 19. Bakke, a church historian, provides a much more nuanced discussion of these issues in Jewish antiquity (*When Children Became People*, 110–14, and corresponding endnotes).

10. Thompson, "Children in the Gospel of John," 205.

cultural practices such as infanticide, exposure, and sale or debt-bondage represented malicious threats to children by adults. Infanticide, the deliberate killing of infants and young children, or its attempt is attested in Jewish sources.[11] The Isaac narrative is perhaps the most obvious example. Although unconsummated, it has been recently noted that the narrative is haunted thereafter by a sense of estrangement; Abraham and Isaac never again converse.[12] Perhaps more indicative of actual practice, a number of passages suggest child sacrifice was not unknown among the ancient Israelites.[13] For example, it may have been the following commandment from Exodus that led to Israelite practices which Ezekiel found so offensive:

> Your firstborn sons you shall give to me. You shall do the same with your oxen and with your sheep: it shall be with its mother seven days; you must give it over to me on the eighth day. (Exod 22:29b-30)[14]

---

11. On this matter, I concur with historian John Boswell that there is a necessary distinction between infanticide and abandonment. The latter does not necessarily result in the former, yet the two are most often conflated. Their distinction is very important, since abandonment "was the *alternative* to infanticide in much of Europe"; parents knew that abandoned children were frequently taken in by others, even if under less than desirable circumstances. According to Boswell, "[T]he frequency of infanticide and abandonment in societies where both were common indicate that abandonments outnumbered infanticides by factors ranging from several hundred to nearly a thousand. Killing children is, moreover, not only morally different from leaving them in a place where they might be picked up and reared; it also entails dramatically different consequences. If even a small percentage of abandoned children were rescued, abandonment would have a less drastic effect on the next generation than an equal rate of infanticide" (Boswell, *Kindness*, 44–45). Boswell's discussion is very helpful in these distinctions. However, most scholars who tend to conflate infanticide and abandonment, and Boswell too, fall short in their treatments of infanticide. The killing of infants and young children is not limited to one's own children in ancient texts, or modern society for that matter. Infants are killed, deliberately or as "collateral damage," in warfare, in judgments by authorities, and in other contexts. The argument that the ancient Canaanite/Phoenicians engaged in large scale infant sacrifice, based on the high number of infant remains in burial urns at the Tophet in Carthage, has recently been challenged by archaeological analysis. Lobell, "Child Burials."

12. Fretheim, "God Was with the Boy," 14–23.

13. For example, Lev 18:21 and 20:2–5 are prescriptive, and could represent responses to practices among the population considered abominable. 2 Kgs 23:10, 2 Chron 28:3 and 33:6 are examples of accusations against a ruling party and could be either fictitious polemic or represent some sense of reality. Jer 19:5; 32.35 and Ezekiel 16:20–21; and 23:37–39 can be read as accusations against some element of the people of Israel and Judah more broadly, but at least as an accusation against their ruling classes.

14. The offspring of both humans and animals are encapsulated in this command

Was child sacrifice more common (a very relative term) among ancient Israelites than we would like to think? Is this why so many other passages in Torah and the prophets railed against this practice? Meanwhile, children often taunt, hurling "childish" epithets at others. Yet, forty-two boys were massacred, implicitly by divine retribution, in 1 Kgs 2:23–24 for calling Elisha "baldhead."[15] Just as startling are references to killing and/or consuming one's children.[16] In fact, one of the most gruesome descriptions in all of ancient literature is the pitiful story of the two mothers who agreed to cook and eat their sons, only for one mother to renege (2 Kings 6:28–29).[17]

There are also stories of, or allusions to, abandonment in Jewish tradition. Abraham abandons Ishmael to the desert. The birth motif of Moses also preserves an abandonment scene, which has been turned into an account of divine preservation (Exod 2).[18] Ezekiel uses the metaphor of an abandoned child in his portrayal of God's relationship with Israel:

> Thus says the LORD God to Jerusalem . . . .. As for your birth, on the day you were born your navel cord was not cut, nor were you washed with water to clean you, nor rubbed with salt, nor wrapped in receiving cloths. No eye felt sorry for you, to do any of these things out of compassion for you; but you were cast away in the open field, for you were detested on the day you were born. I passed by you, and saw you kicking about in your blood. As you lay in your blood, I said to you, "Live! and grow like a plant of the field." You developed and became tall and arrived at full womanhood. (Ezek 16:3a, 4–7b)

As historian John Boswell puts it, "The image would seem to lack force if abandoned children were not a familiar part of life among those to whom

---

and there is no suggestion here that exempts the human baby for redemption. See Ezek 20:25–26, 31a for his comments.

15. Compare infanticide as divine punishment in 2 Sam 12:15 and Jephthah's slaughter of his daughter, Judg 11:29–40.

16. For example, as one of the results of breaking the covenant, the god of Israel pledges in Lev 26:29 "You shall eat the flesh of your sons, and you shall eat the flesh of your daughters." Deut 28:53–56 places this curse in the context of a siege upon the land by an enemy. The resulting famine and starvation is promised to result in cannibalism.

17. For other passages, see Jer 19:9; Ezek 5:10; Lam 2:20.

18. Recounting the story of Moses in Acts 7, Stephen tells the High Priest and council, "At this time Moses was born . . .; and when he was abandoned, Pharaoh's daughter adopted him, and brought him up as her own son" (Acts 2:20a, 21; NRSV). Portrayed in this manner, the author of Acts narrowly construes the account as one of abandonment.

it was directed."[19] Additionally, abandonment may be implied in the forced breakup of marriages under the post-exilic reforms of Ezra and Nehemiah (Ezra 9–10; Neh 10:30; 13:23–31), and the reference to *asufi* among Jews who returned to Judah from Babylon (*m. Kiddushin* 4:2). In fact, the Babylonian Talmud deals with the problem of abandonment in several places.[20]

Neither were the ancient Israelites or their god exceptional from their contemporaries when in it came to the plight of children during war. The lives of all firstborn males were demanded by the divine warriors of both Egypt and Israel.[21] For the Deuteronomist, enemy children captured from towns far away are a prize of war, to be exploited as slaves. But of the enemy within, in direct contestation for the land, including their children, Deuteronomy records "you must not let anything that breathes remain alive. You shall annihilate them" (20:16–17, NRSV).[22]

This perusal through Jewish literature suggests there is also a dark side to child history within Jewish sources. Although Jewish sources are much less explicit about infanticide and exposure among their own than Greco-Roman sources, the practices were obviously not unknown among Jews before the introduction of Hellenism, and probably took place despite legal prescriptions to the contrary.[23]

19. Boswell, *Kindness*, 146. Boswell also cites Hanna's relinquishing of Samuel to the priest at Shiloh as abandonment (ibid., 147), broadly interpreted, which in my opinion technically fits the notion since abandonment in both Jewish and Greco-Roman antiquity did not always imply certain death. Even more unsettling, Ezekiel's full allegory in chapter sixteen depicts an adult male (God) that takes in the foundling girl (Jerusalem). Now her father, he raises and "adorn[s]" her for his own sexual pleasures, only to find that she "lavished [her] whorings on any passer-by" (Ezek 16:15, NRSV)! As a result, God satisfies his "fury" and "jealousy" by permitting what at first appears to be the initial stages of a gang rape by her lovers, then punishes her by public stoning (16:35–42).

20. The quotation of *m. Kiddushin* 4:2 is from Cooper, *Child*, 40. For the full discussion of abandonment in the Mishnah and Babylonian Talmud, see ibid., 40–41. Also Bakke, *When Children Became People*, 114.

21. McGinnis, "Exodus," 30–37. Cf. Wisdom of Solomon 18:5, 10, 12–13: "When they had decided to kill the infants (νήπια) of your holy ones, and one child had been abandoned and rescued, you deprived them of a multitude of their children in punishment . . . But the disagreeable cry of their enemies resounded, and their pathetic cry for their children was spread abroad . . . since at one moment their precious children had been destroyed . . . when their firstborn were destroyed, they acknowledged your people to be God's υἱὸν" ("son" or "child"). As for the overall subject of abandonment, broadly construed, the child Samuel could be considered abandoned (1 Sam 1:24–28) as Joseph, who was in the charge of his older brothers (Gen 37:19–28).

22. Cf. Ps 137:9.

23. For a good overview of these problems in Jewish society, see Cooper, *Child*,

In spite of such challenges to the paradigmatic view, children played an essential role in the ideological importance of family in Jewish tradition. In fact, "without the presence of children, God would be impotent to fulfill his promises of inheritance and blessing."[24] Ideologically for parents and caregivers, Jewish children were valued because they represented one sign that the covenant between the Jewish people and their god was still alive.[25] And it was just as important during the Hellenistic-Roman period to reiterate God's promise through retellings of Israelite history that included God's favor in spite of barrenness or threats to Israel's children.[26]

However, there is little evidence in Jewish sources of this period that children were valued *as children*. Prophetic passages reveal little about how real caregivers actually felt about children born to them (e.g., Ezek 37:25; Isa 9:6; 59:21).[27] References to orphans at the least seem to refer to those without a father, and so young children can be assumed, but dependent adolescents may not be excluded either (Exod 22:21–22).[28] Instead, children in Jewish traditions are almost always portrayed as significant for how they will function as adult children. In other words, Jewish boys were functionally significant as heirs that will inherit the land, their family's social status, and maintain the covenant with their god. Jewish girls were functionally significant for their future role as mothers and their help to maintain the family's covenant with God. Both were prized as caretakers of elderly parents.[29]

35–44, and Boswell, *Kindness*, 139–52.

24. Murphy, Review of *Child in the Bible*, 3–4.

25. Carroll, "Children in the Bible," 124; Horn and Martens, *Let the Little Children Come*, 45–46; Jensen, *Graced Vulnerability*, 2–3. Conversely, among the terrible results of Adam's transgression, the author of 2 Baruch lists: begetting children and the passion of parents (2 Baruch 56:6).

26. E.g., Jubilees 28:11–24; 47:2; 48:14

27. Contra Perdue's positive statements (Perdue, "Israelite," 171) and Jensen's assertion, "Compared with many . . ., Israel valued and welcomed children wholeheartedly," (*Graced Vulnerability*, 2–3). Meanwhile, one must note that the *Laws of Hammurabi* contains an entire section (33.78—34.6; 34.74—37.60) concerned with the welfare of children. *The Story of Ahikar* 2.28 implies young children are highly valued, because the lack of children is a sign of disgrace and contempt before one's enemies.

28. Compare Jensen's treatment (*Graced Vulnerability*, 3). Again, divine law codes of ancient Mesopotamia show a similar concern to protect and provide for orphans (see the *Laws of Ur-Namma* A.4.162–68).

29. See the entirety of Tobit, but especially 3:12 and 4:3–4; also Philo, *Decal.* 116–19 (cf. Aristotle, *Ethica nicomachea* 1165a 21–27); *Sibylline Oracles* 2:27274–275; Reinhartz,

Traditionally, male children represented heirs that carried on their ancestral way of life and property, whether pastoral, agricultural, fishing, or commercial, and a natural or adopted son could function in this role (Genesis 12, 15–16, 18, 21; Matt 4:21).[30] For instance, the Book of Tobit hinges on the struggle of two families to secure the marriage of Tobit's son, Tobias, to Raguel's daughter, Sarah, whereby Tobias "inherited the house of Raguel and of Tobit his father" (14:13). Sons were expected to maintain or further their family's honor publically, as well as its proper covenant relationship with God by learning and observing Torah and through proper worship.[31]

For girls, the expectation to maintain the family's covenant relationship with God was inextricably bound to their significance as future mothers. In other words, nearly the entire functional emphasis placed upon girls in this period concerns the maintenance of sexual purity until marriage, so that they might bear legitimate heirs for their husbands. Jesus ben Sira obsesses over the potentially shameful sexuality of daughters, whether young or already married (Sir 7:23–25; 22:4–6; 26:10–12; 42:9–14). In Tobit, the young Sarah is introduced as a distressed young Jewish woman who fails seven times to secure an heir for her father. Yet, the author stresses clearly that none of her seven failed marriages were sexually consummated (3:8). Therefore, her primary role of maintaining sexual purity until she bore legitimate heirs was realized. In Luke, the birth of a son named John reportedly "took away the disgrace [Elizabeth] endured" amidst her peers (1:25), while Mary's entire purpose was seemingly to become the virgin mother of Jesus (1:27, 34, 46–55).[32]

Reared almost exclusively in the woman's sphere, children probably began engaging in tasks as early as five or six, such as gathering firewood, picking food, spinning and weaving, or attending toddlers. By maturation, twelve to thirteen, children engaged in gender-specific tasks. Boys were introduced into the harsh demands of the adult male world and apprenticed in their father's trade; girls increasingly took on the harsher and

"Parents and Children," 80–81; Perdue, "Israelite," 190.

30. For example, on Levirate marriage, see Mark 12:18–27; cf. Matt 22:23–32; Luke 20:27–40. On certain Essene groups securing children for spiritual heirs, see Josephus, *B.J.* 2.8.120. For further discussion, see Perdue, "Israelite," 187–88.

31. In one sense, the extensive advice directed to "my child" throughout the entire Book of Sirach can be construed in this manner. On a son's role in maintaining a family and kin-group's social status, see Neyrey, *Honor and Shame*, 14–32, and deSilva, *Honor*, 23–42.

32. Collins, "Marriage," 142–43.

more complex duties of adult female labor, perhaps as brides within a new household.[33] Meanwhile, Jewish wisdom literature lays tremendous stress on education and the strict discipline necessary for becoming a virtuous man.[34]

Throughout the scope of Jewish literature, children are almost exclusively characterized or spoken of within the context of households or families.[35] In most cases this seems to be a sedentary existence, i.e., they existed as part of a family set within a settled community, such as a rural village or a city.[36] It is probably safe to assume that children also lived within nomadic or commercial families, where the norm may have consisted of periods of settle existence in one locale broken by frequent travel to another because of the economic processes upon which the household existed, e.g., pastoral or commercial livelihoods.

By whatever means the family existed, children lived in relation to, *and dependent upon*, caregivers or other adults who tend to be more important to the educated, elite group of writers that have left us with traces of their presence in the stories and traditions of antiquity. At least in a prescriptive sense, children raised by Jewish caregivers became part of the covenant community, albeit with gender differences.[37] They were a fundamental part of some of the communities represented among the Dead Sea Scrolls, where they were to be carefully raised in strictest observations of the law.

> When they come, they shall assemble all those who come, including children and women, and they shall read into [their] ea[rs] all the precepts of the covenant, and shall instruct them in all their regulations, so that they do not stray in [the]ir e[rrors] . . . From [his] yo[uth] [they shall edu]cate him in the book of HAGY, and

33. Meyers, "Family in Early Israel," 27; Pilch, "'Beat His Ribs,'" 104–5.

34. Sir 3:1–15; Philo, *Hypoth.* 8.7.14; *Jub* 39:6; 4 Macc 18:10–19; Josephus, *C. Ap.* 2.25.204; b. *Šabb.* 12a; *m. Hag.* 1.1; and *m. Meg.* 4.5–6. See Yarbrough, "Parents and Children," 47. Pseudepigraphal works are taken from Charlesworth, *Pseudepigrapha*.

35. The only distinction I make between the two is that families consist of the men and women, caregivers and children, masters and slaves, or any other relationship between persons within a household. A household, as I construe it, includes these relationships and the additional material property that belongs to the head of the household, including animals, equipment, and sometimes land.

36. Safrai, "Home and Family," 728–29. See also Collins, "Marriage," 105–6 for the emerging importance of the *bêt 'ābôt* during the Second Temple period.

37. On circumcision of boys, see Gen 17:12; Lev 12:3; 1 Macc 1:60. On the participation of boys and girls in community-wide ceremonies, see Exod 12:26–27; Deut 4:9–10; 29:11; Ezra 10:1.

according to his age, instruct him in the precept[s of] the covenant, and he will [receive] his [ins]struction in their regulations;
during ten years he will be counted among the children. At the
a[ge] of twenty ye[ars, he will] . . . join the holy commun[ity].
(1QSa I.4–9)[38]

Meanwhile, in terms aspects of daily life such as play, John Cooper lists a
few studies and excavations from the Levant that discuss what some have
interpreted as toys.[39]

There were, of course, other forms of childhood within Jewish tradition, such as slave or orphaned children, less attested, but which were
no less dependent upon life in some form of familial structure. According
to Exodus 21:7–11, fathers could sell their children into debt-servitude or
slavery (cf. 2 Kgs 4:1). Should a debt-slave have children while in his master's charge, they belonged to the master once he became free (Exod 21:2–
11). A Jewish father could sell his daughter into concubinage, in which she
remained for life, or at the discretion of her owner. As such, her primary
task was sexual and the production of children. However, debt-slavery of
Jews among Jews appears to have been prohibited, at least in theory, in the
post-exilic period (Lev 25:39–46).[40] Jews were also permitted to make or
buy slaves, including children, from non-Jews who lived among them, and
the children of foreign slaves could be left as property to one's own children
(Lev 25:44–46; Eccles 2:7).

There were also children orphaned by war or by the dissolution of
families through divorce, or became fatherless for one reason or another.[41]

38. Cf. 1QM VII.3–4; CD-A VII.6–7; XV 5–6; 4Q502. Also see *Fragments of a
Zadokite Work* 9.1 in Charles, *Pseudepigrapha*. CD-A XV.16 appears to bar under age
boys from entering the congregation, but this may only point to their exclusion from a
ceremonial rank within the community, since the context refers to those who are tested
by the "Inspector of the Many." English translation of 1QSa above is from Martínez and
Tigchelaar, *Dead Sea Scrolls*; see also Schofield, *From Qumran to the Yahad*.

39. Also note passages that attest to children at play such as Matt 11:16–17; Jer 6:11;
Zech 8:5. The latter two sources date prior to the Hellenistic period, as do some of the
artifacts interpreted as toys, but cautiously we might assume they testify to a normative
desire on the part of children to play, and some acquiescence among parents, at least of
urban settings to permit it (Cooper, *Child*, 19).

40. Cf. 2 Chron 28:8–15. For a general discussion of the biblical history of debt-
servitude, see Perdue, "Israelite," 195–97. The Law also made provision for the redemption of slaves by a kinsman.

41. Perdue footnotes a study that suggests some fatherless may be offspring of
cultic prostitutes. See Perdue, "Israelite," 193, 219nn85–86.

Yet, numerous texts within earlier Jewish tradition call for their support and protection (Exod 22:21–25; Deut 14:28–29; 16:9–11, 13–14; 24:17, 19–21; 27:19). The prophets frequently excoriated those that oppressed orphans and charged the righteous to come to their aid (Isa 1:17, 23; 9:17; 10:1–2; Jer 5:28; 22:3; Zech 7:10; Mal 3:5). And wisdom texts promote their cause (e.g., Prov 23:10). These texts are prescriptive, and do not necessarily attest to reality. Perhaps there were, in reality, homeless and neglected persons, even street children, within the context of Hellenistic-Roman Palestine, or within Jewish communities of the Diaspora. We simply cannot tell. Within the extant texts, children appear only to exist under the charge of some caretaker, whether a parent, priest, or slave-master.

Meanwhile, since Jesus' "remarkable display of love and affection" has been characterized as more in line with Jewish than Hellenistic attitudes toward children,[42] is there much evidence of affection or sentimentality toward children in Jewish tradition? First, in support, Gundry asserts: "We find, first of all, testimonies to parental love and pleasure in children, such as 4 Maccabees 15:4 [. . .] and anecdotes suggesting the same."[43] Because this entire section reflects on a mother's emotions over the martyrdom of her seven sons, for our purposes, a handful of verses from chapter fifteen are worth quoting.

> O reason of children, tyrant over the emotions, and religion, longed for more than her children by their mother! Two paths were open to this mother, that of religion, and that of saving her seven sons for a time, as the tyrant had promised. She loved religion more, which saves them for eternal life according to God's promise. How might I express the emotions of parents who love their children? We inscribe upon the character of a little child an amazing image both of mind and of form. This is truer of mothers than fathers because their labor pains foster a greater sympathy toward their children . . . they are more committed to their children. The mother of the seven boys loved her children more than any other mother. Through seven pregnancies she had stirred in herself tender love toward them . . . and [they] loved their brothers and their mother, so that they obeyed her even to death in keeping the ordinances . . . O sacred nature and affection of parental love,

42. Gundry, "Children," 157.

43. Gundry, "Least and the Greatest," 34. Also Carroll, "Children in the Bible," 122; Francis, "Children and Childhood," 71 (my emphasis). Also in support, Perdue asserts, "Tenderness, love, and affection for children are often expressed in the Hebrew Bible, as is the sustaining care provided to children" (Perdue, "Israelite," 171).

the longing of parents toward children, nurture and unassailable
suffering by mothers! (4 Macc 15:1–13)

The passage, which goes on for some time in this manner, is the most
sentimental expression of the love of a parent for her children in Jewish
literature of the period. It is a beautiful elaboration of 2 Maccabees 7:1–42.
Second, Adele Reinhartz notes that Philo argues that "love and affection,"
particularly of parents toward children, is an implicit part of parenthood.[44]
Finally, R. Simeon b. Judah from the *Pirke Aboth* states that "children are
comely for the righteous and comely for the world; . . . Children's children
are the crown of old men; and the glory of children are their fathers" (6.8).[45]

However, before we acquiesce to assertions that such evidence shows
Jews valued more or were more affectionate toward children than the
cultures around them, some criticism of the evidence is necessary. First,
although Philo speaks of the naturalness of such affections, he does so as a
philosopher. So far as we can tell, he is not describing observations of affection. In fact, a running theme within Philo is his passion for wisdom and
reason and his corresponding circumspection about the natural world and
fleshly existence. Therefore, among other things, children and the time and
care they demand "withers wisdom before it blooms" (*Gig.* 30). Of course,
children are not the problem for Philo. Rather, it is the flesh's demand for
pleasure, which enslaves.

> For he who is bound by the love charms of his wife, or compelled
> by nature puts his children first, is no longer the same to others,
> but unconsciously has become another person, a slave apart from
> freedom. (*Hypoth.* 11.17)[46]

It is for this reason that Philo so admires communal groups such as the
Therapeutae of Egypt and the Essenes of Palestine, among whom he takes
celibacy to be the norm (*Hypoth.* 11.3). Philo is not singing the virtues of
affection on behalf of Jewish parents for their children so much as simply
stating what he believes to be a natural "pleasure" for the human caregiver
of children. It is because he views such passions as natural that he can

44. Philo, *Spec.* 2.239, 240. Philo also characterizes Abraham as one who admirably
withheld emotion as he prepared to sacrifice his son, although "devoted to his son with a
fondness which no words can express" (*Abr.* 169). This stoic demeanor was an unnatural
expression, "for parents somehow dote on their late-born children" (*Abr.* 195). See also
De Iosepho 4 (Reinhartz, "Parents and Children," 81–85).

45. Cf. Prov 17:6.

46. Also see *Opif.* 161.

castigate those who seem to him to be dispassionate toward children as unnatural. In other words, those who do not care for children and dispose of them in some way are criticized by one who finds marriage, children, and the daily concerns of this world a hindrance to the pursuit of wisdom.[47]

Similarly, the author of 4 Maccabees is actually extolling the virtues of reason over emotions. From the same account mentioned above, the author characterizes the mother who watched the cruel torture and death of her sons.

> Nor did you cry when you saw the eyes of each [son] in his tortures . . . When you saw the flesh of children . . . you did not cry . . . But giving her heart male fortitude in the midst of her emotions, devout reason strengthened her to overlook her parental love for the duration . . . But if a woman, aged and mother of seven sons, experienced watching her children tortured to death, it must be confessed that devout reason is sovereign over the emotions. (4 Macc 15:19–16:1)

In much more concise fashion, the original account in 2 Maccabees 7 depicts the mother as similarly dispassionate and steadfast in her commitment to observe Jewish laws. But this account lacks descriptions of her affection for her sons, save perhaps 7:27–28. These descriptions were added to highlight the contrast between reason and emotion by the author of 4 Maccabees. To frustrate matters more, Robert von Thaden has recently pointed out that children do not fare well generally within the Jewish wisdom tradition.[48] Of course this brief foray into the textual evidence does not prove, nor, one hopes, even suggest, that Jewish parents and children loved each other less than those around them. It simply means there is a paucity of such references in the textual tradition.

Two things should be said in summary. First, children were certainly valued within diverse Jewish populations, perhaps more for their roles as adults, or perhaps that is all the evidence suggests to this point. Certainly we are disadvantaged by Jewish legal restrictions on images. Despite the fact that both Philo and the author of 4 Maccabees are more concerned with the virtues of wisdom and reason than the day-to-day relationships of family, their writings nevertheless testify that affection between caregivers and children are assumed to be a natural aspect of their relationships. To

---

47. Here, I am indebted to Robert H. von Thaden, who was kind enough to send me a copy of a 2008 conference paper. Thaden, "Thinking with Children," 5.

48. Ibid.

suggest, as some have, that Jews loved or valued children more (or less) than other cultures, and hang the argument on a lack of contraception, abortion,[49] infanticide, or exposure among Jews merely oversimplifies the evidence for the sake of a theological purpose. Such assertions betray more about our own interests and agendas than they can tell us about how much a given culture valued something. A better assertion might be that, in some ways, Jews or Jewish tradition valued (and devalued) children differently than surrounding cultures, but similarly in several ways.

Second, children may have existed in a wide array of conditions in the Jewish world of the period under examination, but they were ever under the care and supervision of one or more caretakers. Boys and girls were raised in sheltered environments, largely under the watchful eyes of women until they were old enough to be tasked with some duties. Covenant children, particularly males, were educated in Jewish Law and traditions. Girls were increasingly taught the necessities of domestic work, such as food gathering and preparation, and were prepared for eventual marriage. As they aged, boys and girls, free or slave, were tasked with more gender-specific duties. Nonetheless, whether orphaned or fatherless, a slave or debt-servant, boy or girl, *children were almost always dependent upon, and situated within, a structured family setting.*

Children in the Hellenistic-Roman World

As in the Jewish tradition, there is also evidence that shows the value of children in Hellenistic and Roman societies. Xenophon, the early fourth-century Greek playwright, says that procreation was the principal reason for marriage (*Oeconomicus* 7.12).[50] Unlike Genesis, there is no central governing mythos among Greco-Romans to provide a single prescriptive theological reason for bearing children. In one sense, having children was simply a given. It is what couples do, as Cicero assumed in a letter to his son ca. 46 BCE,

> Since it is a natural inclination of all living things that they have the instinct to reproduce, the first association is that of marriage; the next is with one's children; then the household . . .; that is . . . as it were the seed-bed of the state. (*De Officiis* 1.54–55)

49. Again, I shall deal with these arguments at a later time.
50. Also Lacey, *Family*.

Nevertheless, there were times when the value of children was raised at the highest levels of society, and some aspect of their importance was affirmed in law. For example, Pericles' citizenship law of 451 BCE attests that children were essential for Athenians to perpetuate their free citizenry and their territorial integrity.[51] Similarly in Rome, legislation was formulated by Caesar Augustus[52] that attempted to increase the number of children born to aristocratic families of Rome.[53] To some degree, however, there was always a blending of state concerns with procreation in Rome. Dixon recounts how, during the census, Roman censors customarily asked men of equestrian and senatorial ranks: "Have you married *for the purpose of creating children*?" It is a widely attested phrase over time and genre of literature, lending force to its currency among Romans in both official and popular arenas.[54] At the most basic level of the household, children were vital in large agrarian societies such as Greece and Rome for their roles as heir of the family estate and property. As Golden puts it, "Children were a prudent investment in a society that knew no pension plans and in which burial and tendance of the grave were important responsibilities of one's descendants."[55] For Romans, Dio's presentation of Augustus' remarks shows

51. Ibid., 100–106.

52. The *Lex Papia Poppaea* was introduced by the two consuls in 18 BCE, but apparently devised by Augustus. The latter introduced the *Lex Iulia* himself in 9 CE. Dixon, *Roman Family*, 79, 209n85.

53. Dixon, *Roman Family*, 80. Whether Augustus merely acted to restore some nostalgic perception of Rome's glorified past, or whether he acted to stay a perceived demographic problem among the aristocracy, the legislation never produced the desired results. According to Tacitus, childlessness strongly prevailed among this demographic (*Annales* 3.25). The effect, however, was that Roman families emerged out of a largely private sphere into broader public scrutiny. By the early second century CE, a public *alimenta* system was instituted under the emperor Trajan whereby the Roman state distributed public funds for the support of Italian infants and children (Rawson, "Adult-Child Relationships," 23; Dixon, *Roman Family*, 121, 124).

54. Dixon gleans this formula from a number of texts: Valerius Maximus, *Factorum et dictorum memorabilium* 7.7.4; Aulus Gellius, *Noct. att.* 4.3.2; 17.21.44; Livy, *Ep.* 59; and Suetonius, *Caes.* 52.3. Within her text, she also cites a character in a play by the early second-century BCE playwright Plautus which tells her brother, "I want you to marry a wife so that you can procreate children—may the gods grant it!" (Plautus, *Aul.* 146–49). She also cites similar expressions in a marriage contract from the time of Augustus, and similar attestations by St. Augustine in his day (Dixon, *Roman Family*, 67–68, and nn28–31; my emphasis). See also a speech, purportedly delivered by Augustus to members of the Roman aristocracy in conjunction with his legislation, presented in Dio Cassius, *Hist. rom.* 56.3.

55. Golden, *Children and Childhood*, 93.

not only children's significance as heirs, but also conveys a sense of concern and sentiment about them.

> Is it not a joy to acknowledge a child who possesses the qualities of both parents, to tend and educate a person who is both the physical and mental mirror of yourself, so that, as he [or she] grows up, another self is created? Is it not a blessing, when we leave this life, to leave behind as our successor an heir both to our family and to our property, one that is our own, born of our own essence, so that only the mortal part of us passes away, while we live on in the child who succeeds us? (Dio Cassius *Hist. rom.* 56.3)[56]

Beyond this ontological form of discussion for children, what did they mean to or for Hellenistic and Roman parents and caregivers in the period of our study? Is there evidence they were valued as children, or merely for the roles they would assume as adults? Is there evidence of affection or sentimentality for children? How rooted in and dependent on their families were children in the Hellenistic-Roman world, and is there evidence to suggest children acted autonomously to become learners in prophetic circles or of philosophic or religious schools?

There seems to exist among scholars on children in the biblical world a general assertion that Greeks and Romans valued children much less than Jews. Most of this assessment derives from those issues which surround birth and acceptance of children into the family, and although for brevity's sake, I shall discuss issues of contraception and abortion elsewhere, I shall presently address issues of infanticide and exposure.

Infanticide is also attested in Greco-Roman sources, although as already mentioned, scholars often conflate it with abandonment.[57] In terms of the family, much has been made of the Roman father's power *patria potestas*, particularly his right to accept or reject newborns into the family. Rejection typically meant *expositio*, or abandonment, of the newborn, but this did not always result in death. Sometimes it was rescued and raised as freeborn by another household, raised as a household slave, raised for the slave market, for prostitution, or other reasons. Nevertheless, where infanticide resulted from exposure, it was legal under Roman law until the

---

56. For stylistic purposes, I have chosen here Wiedemann's translation over that of Cary's in the LCL. See Wiedemann, *Adults and Children*, 25; cf. Gardner and Wiedemann, *Roman Household*, 97.

57. For example, Golden, *Children and Childhood*, 86, 90; Oakley, "Death and the Child," 178–79.

fourth century CE.[58] Cicero states that the Twelve Tables affirmed that any child born with some defect or deformity should be killed quickly (*De Legibus* 3.19).[59] Later, in his legal records, the second-century Roman lawyer and magistrate Ulpian decrees that parents of such children should take pleasure in their right to have them (*ius liberorum*; *Dig.* 50.16.135). Nevertheless, not all instances of *expositio* that resulted in death were due to deformity. Raising children was costly and could be burdensome, especially to the poor.[60] And much has been made of the first-century BCE letter of Hilarion to his wife, Alis, recovered from Oxyrhynchus, Egypt. It is often cited as conveying *the* "pagan attitude" toward newborns.

> I beg and entreat you, take care of the little one, and as soon as we receive our pay I will send it up to you. If by chance you bear a child, if it is a boy, let it be, if it is a girl, expose it. (*P. Oxy.* 744).[61]

Of course the Hellenistic and Roman worlds were quite diverse with opinion. We may not know what would have been acceptable or unacceptable if pressed to elaborate, but the Latin writer Publilius Syrus declares in one of his sayings: "He who kills a child is cruel, not brave" (*Maxims* 49.123).[62]

---

58. See the descriptions in Dionysius of Halicarnassus, *Roman Antiquities* 2.15. Yet, Boswell notes that Dionysius contradicts himself, where he explicitly says in 9.22 that Romans are to rear *all* children. Boswell further notes that Dionysius' statements are based on "no known source, written seven centuries after the alleged event, and supported by no other documentation, legal, historical, or literary" (Boswell, *Kindness*, 59). The reference of Dionysius aside, Boswell further notes that Romans were nowhere legally required to raise any of their children. This is because Roman law was concerned with peoples' obligations to the state, or to mitigate disputes over property, status, and injury; it was not overly concerned with the moral behavior of its citizens (ibid., 58–59). Plutarch believed Lycurgus instituted the deliberate killing of deformed or unhealthy newborns among the ancient Spartans (*Lycurgus* 16.1–2).

59. Compare Seneca, *De ira* 1.15.2: "*portentosos fetus exstinguimus, liberos quoque, si debiles monstrosique editi sunt, mergimus*" (Unnatural progeny, we destroy; we drown even children who at birth are weakly and abnormal). English translation from LCL.

60. Ovid gives a pitiful, perhaps not to unrealistic illustration of a father's decision to condemn to death a newborn, citing their poverty as the reason: "When [Ligdus'] pregnant wife was near giving birth, he said to her, 'There are two things that I wish: that your labour may be easy, and that your child will be a boy. A daughter is too expensive, and we do not have the resources. With great regret I have to say that if it should be a girl, we will have to let her die.' When he finished, tears washed both the face of the man who gave the order, and the woman to whom it was given" (*Metamorphoses* 9.669–681); Gardner and Wiedemann, *Roman Household*, 98.

61. Cited in Ferguson, *Backgrounds*, 74.

62. Translation taken from Gardner and Wiedemann, *Roman Household*, 46.

In addition to infanticide *within* the realm of the family, children are sometimes cited as victims of war or political intrigue. The Gospel of Matthew tells us that in King Herod's desperation over the birth of a rival for his throne, he killed all of the children around two years and under in the town of Bethlehem (2:16).[63] Josephus cites numerous examples of the slaughter of infants and children caught in the throes of war (*Ant.* 14.480; *B.J.* 2.306–07). He invokes his fellow Jewish fighters to envision the slaughter that would also include their children at the hands of the Romans at Jotapata should they fail to fight (*B.J.* 3.261).[64] However, a close reading of Josephus reveals a certain "political correctness" in his retelling of historical events under the auspices of his Flavian patrons. He shrewdly makes the point that Vespasian slew all of the hold outs seized in his conquest of Jotapata, *except the women and children* (*B.J.* 3.336). In fact, with respect to the Flavian campaigns against the Jews, Josephus makes it clear that any deaths of women and children were not the direct result of Roman sword, but rather the effects of the refusal of the Jews to surrender.[65] There is also reason to believe that Josephus' accounts of infanticide may not reflect historical reality. His works are replete with the phrases "women and children" and "wives and children," too numerous to list. The saturation of his texts with these common refrains suggests they are more a rhetorical device for Josephus, regardless of their historical veracity. In the texts important to this study, these phrases appear to be used to emphasize the savage nature of some group in comparison to another, i.e., combatants are morally evaluated by how the weakest members of society are treated.[66]

In addition, our sources attest that Greeks and Romans sometimes practiced *expositio,* or abandonment of newborns. As biblical scholars, it can appear that we highlight this factor for its shock value, as if to emphasize how much more wretched pagans (or *Gentiles*) treated children.

63. This might be a literary account meant to show the fulfillment of Jer 31:15 and also echo the Exodus account, rather than a record of an actual historical event. Josephus gives no corroborating account in his hostile witness to Herod's reign. Yet its inclusion in Matthew's narrative anticipates that readers at least find the literary events and motifs plausible.

64. Compare Josephus' account of his speech to his countrymen on behalf of Titus, to dissuade them from resisting Rome's advance on Jerusalem (*B.J.* 5.418).

65. For example, Josephus goes to lengths to describe the deplorable starvation of children and others as a result of the Flavian siege of Jerusalem (*B.J.* 5.430, 433, 513; 6.205–11; 7.389–400). Were these results due to Jewish obstinacy or Roman military determination? Josephus implicitly suggests the former.

66. Cf. Josephus, *B.J.* 3.262–63.

However, in truth we have very little idea how common or uncommon the practice was during the Hellenistic and early Roman imperial periods. In his monograph *Children and Childhood in Classical Athens*, historian Mark Golden states: "Now, it is likely (though not beyond a reasonable doubt) that the exposure of newborns, especially newborn girls, was widespread and even common at Athens."[67] But his primary discussion is over whether Athenian parents cared for children in spite of such practices, a subject which I shall return to in this chapter.[68] Greek sources assume its practice in the classical period.[69] Abandonment in the ancient Roman world has been documented extensively by historian John Boswell, who argues it was not only common, but a typical family practice. However, most of these children were immediately taken and nurtured, with the result that they suffered mortality little different from children reared in their natal families.[70] Yet, Boswell's sources focus principally on foundlings, which may skew his analysis. It is simply impossible to tell how many exposed children died versus how many survived.

References to exposure are scattered among our extant Roman sources. Some are fictitious, set within mythological or folk tales.[71] Others are referenced within legal codes.[72] Some are within letters seeking legal guidance, as this second-century exchange between the younger Pliny and the emperor Trajan attests. Pliny writes:

> A serious problem, Sir, which affects the whole province [Bythnia in Asia Minor], concerns the status and cost of maintenance of the persons generally known as foundlings [θρεπτούς]. (*Epistulae* 10.65.1)

And Trajan replies:

67. Golden, *Children and Childhood*, 87.

68. See also Golden, "Demography," 316–31.

69. Plato alludes to it in the discourse between Socrates and Theodoros (*Theaetetus* 160–61). Aristophanes refers to the practice, and also attests to the belief that exposed infants were sometimes taken in by others and raised, even educated (*Nubes* 530–32). And Aristotle also mentions exposure among his discussion of rearing children (*Pol.* 7.16).

70. Boswell, *Kindness*.

71. E.g, Ovid, *Metamorphoses* 9.669–81; also note that the mythological foundations of Rome, the tale of Romulus and Remus, involved their abandonment on the Tiber River. Livy, *Historiae ab urbe condita* 1.4; cf. Plutarch, *Romulus* 3–5.

72. E.g., Ulpian, *Dig.* 25.3.5; 40.4.29.

The question you raise of free persons who were exposed at birth [*nati expositi*], but then brought up in slavery by those who rescued them, *has often been discussed*, but I can find nothing in the records of my predecessors which could have applied to all provinces. (*Epistulae* 10.66.1; my emphasis)[73]

The problem here is not the practice of exposure, but that the problems raised by survivors of exposure involved transgressions of the social boundaries of free and slave, or elsewhere, questions of rights to inheritance.[74]

There were opponents of exposure among non-Christian Greco-Romans, chiefly Stoic philosophers. Epictetus, who wrote in the late first and early second century CE, chided Epicurus for teaching that parents should refrain from raising children because their lives often brought such sorrow.

"Let us not raise children," [Epicurus] says. But a sheep does not abandon its young, nor a wolf—but a man should abandon his? What do you want? Would you have us be as foolish as sheep? But they do not abandon their offspring. Would you have us as wild as wolves? But they do not abandon, either. Come—who will follow your advice seeing his child fallen on the ground crying? Yet, I believe even if your mother and father had surmised that you would say such things, they would not have abandoned you! (*Diatribai* 1.23)

Here, Epictetus stands out by raising the notion that parental responsibility is inherent in nature.[75] Despite such appeals, the second-century Stoic Hierocles clearly felt that most of his contemporaries did not share such concerns (Strobaeus 4.24.14). However, even these writers do not argue one should raise every child born. Rather, they are arguing against the prevailing culture of family planning and limitation.[76]

More importantly though, and often given scant attention by biblical scholars, are the social reasons for all such practices. First, for many

---

73. Pliny, *Epistulae.*

74. See also Eyben, "Family Planning," 5–82; Boswell, "Exposition and *Oblatio*," 10–33.

75. Meanwhile, Musonius Rufus attempted to answer the question, εἰ πάντα τὰ γινόμενα τέκνα θρεπτέον, by addressing the economic problems involved in having several children, for the poor and wealthy. For the poor he crafted an analogy from little birds such as larks, swallows, blackbirds, and nightingales, which have nothing but what they can gather, yet raise all their young. For the wealthy he argues that the presence of siblings is worth far more than material inheritance.

76. Boswell, *Kindness*, 86–87.

families, it may have been economically unfeasible to raise every child that would survive birth and its first several days of life outside the womb. It could be difficult enough to exist in the capricious world of the subsistence-based economies of antiquity. There was little insurance against disaster and economic ruin. Therefore, it was imperative to give one's desired children the best advantages possible. Sometimes, to give greater attention and promise of a future meant making the difficult choice of limiting one's family size.[77] Second, abortion or exposure may have been used by some to alleviate concerns over illegitimacy or incest. Third, there is speculation that some instances may have resulted simply from the patriarchal preference for male births, or to weed out babies born with some form of disability. In societies that stressed the importance of males for replenishing the military, coupled with the economic drain of providing a dowry for a girl's wedding, females were very particularly prone to exposure. The reasons just discussed are not meant to make light of the subject at hand. Rather, they are meant to give some sense of cultural context and rationale for the practices, which are vitally important to any such discussion, whether or not our modern sensibilities seek condemnation or justification.

Turning to questions of dependence and affection, children appear fundamentally an interdependent element of familial life, including religious practices, domestic tasks, and education; there is little evidence to suggest they functioned outside the direction of a *pater* or master. As marginal figures in the social world of antiquity, children were viewed as closer to the gods. For this reason, they typically served as acolytes at various religious functions.[78] Summarizing the Greek child's role in household and community, Golden notes that "cult observance is a thread running through the child's life in both the family and community."[79] In fact, one of the most endearing reliefs that capture the central place of children in religion is a fourth-century BCE votive relief from Brauron, now located in the Brauron Archaeological Museum. It depicts a series of worshipers before Artemis: four couples, each with a child of seemingly different ages, from an infant to a child of perhaps seven to ten.[80]

---

77. Boswell, *Kindness*, 84–85, 87.

78. Wiedemann, *Adults and Children*, 25.

79. Golden, *Children and Childhood*, 49.

80. Neils, "Children and Greek Religion," 157, fig. 20. Also, the Oschophoria, an autumn festival, was concerned with the coming of age of Athenian boys, but younger boys probably attended the recitation of stories that were part of the ceremony (Plutarch, *Thes.* 23.3).

The same sentiment also seems applicable to the participation of Roman children in their families' observances. For example, the Daisia, the Attic festival of the serpentine Zeus Meilichius, may have centered on children. The second day of the Anthesteria festival, Choes, which celebrated fertility and abundance in the flowering of spring and new wine, seemed particularly connected with children. *Choes* have been unearthed that depict children engaged in various forms of play.[81]

Meanwhile, religion was a powerful educational force, primarily through the example of adults and their own participation.[82] Young boys and girls were also consecrated for temple service as young acolytes [Latin: *camillus/camilla*] in both Greek and Roman religious rites.[83] For example, Pausanias, a second-century CE travel journalist, mentions the consecration of maidens to Artemis and Poseidon (*Graeciae description* 7.19.1; 7.26.4). Young Athenian girls typically spent a year in service to Artemis at her precinct at Brauron. And boys were consecrated to Apollo at Thebes, to Zeus at Aigion (*Descr.* 7.24.4), and to Athena in Tegea and Elateia (*Descr.* 8.47.3; 10.34.8). Children were also frequently initiated into the Bacchic mysteries, and at the annual festival at Eleusis, a "child from the hearth" was initiated into the mysteries of Demeter (*Hymn. Dem.* 239–91).[84] In addition to literary references, historian Matthew Dillon refers to a number of votive reliefs and statues from the classical period where families, including children are depicted in worship at various temples and shrines.[85] Within the more private confines of the home, young Roman children, and probably also Greek children, served as acolytes for their fathers and mothers during performance of family rites.[86]

---

81. Golden, *Children and Childhood*, 41–44; for illustrations of children on *choes* and in other ritual settings, and for the presence of children in Greek religion generally, see Neils, "Children and Greek Religion," 139–61.

82. As Burkert states: "To honour the gods and to honour one's parents are joint commandments. Plato vividly describes how children, while still at the breast, hear from their mothers and nurses myths which are chanted like spells in sport and in earnest. At sacrifices they hear the prayers and see the corresponding action–magnificent spectacles which children see and hear with such intense delight. Sacrifices are held, and the children see and hear how their parents are engaged for them and for themselves in the greatest seriousness, how they speak to the gods and implore them" (Burkert, *Greek Religion*, 260). The reference to Plato is from *Leg.* 887 de.

83. Burkert, *Greek Religion*, 98.

84. Burkert, *Ancient Mystery Cults*, 52; *Greek Religion*, 288; Mylonas, "Eleusis," 132.

85. Dillon, *Girls and Women*, 31–35.

86. Rose, *Ancient Roman Religion*, 29, 42; Petronius, *Satyricon* 60.

The relationship of young girls to cultic ritual seems to have been more visible, and probably more integrated, within the Greco-Roman world than among Jews. In addition to the depictions of several daughters among the reliefs just mentioned, we have the following verse from Aristophanes' *Lysistrata*, in which women of the chorus sing about their changing religious responsibilities as they emerged from young children to become *parthenoi*.

> Once I was seven I became an arrephoros. Then at ten I became a grain-grinder for the goddess [Artemis]. After that, wearing [?] a saffron robe, I was a bear at Brauron. And, as a lovely young girl, I once served as a basket-bearer, wearing a string of figs. (641–46)[87]

At festivals such as the annual Great Panathenaia, the Dionysia, Epidauria, or the Eleusinia, adolescent girls served as *kanephoroi* [basket-bearers], carrying the essentials such as the sacrificial knife or tuft of barley used in the sacrifice.[88] The east frieze of the Parthenon (slab V, §§31–5) depicts two *arrephoroi* [bearers of sacred things], which appear to be younger or smaller girls than the several *korai* depicted on other pieces of the frieze.[89]

In Rome, the six girls that made up the priesthood of Vestal Virgins were chosen in childhood. Their interstitial status was probably heightened more than most children because of their peculiarly public service in the heart of Rome. These girls maintained the sacred fire at the hearth of Rome, kept and ritually cleaned the sacred storehouse, and prepared the sacred meal (*mola salsa*) from the first pick of the harvest, which was used to bless sacrificial animals. Perhaps most exceptional, for this project, is that they lived together, entirely separate and apparently independent from their real families, in devotion to the goddess and the state.[90]

---

87. Quoted in Neils, "Children and Greek Religion," 149.

88. Neils, "Children and Greek Religion," 152, 158, and figure 21; Dillon, *Girls and Women*, 37–39.

89. The two *arrephoroi* chosen to weave the *peplos* for the grand statue of Athena in the acropolis were undoubtedly aided by several older *parthenoi* in its completion, but their most solemn task was probably carrying the sacred objects during the nocturnal procession of the Arrephoria to the Athenian temple on the acropolis (*Paus.* 1.19.2). About seven years of age, they were specially chosen, and lived on the acropolis near the Athenian temple, serving for one year. How they functioned in relation to their families and the temple are not really known. However, excavators have uncovered a playground on the site (Neils, "Children and Greek Religion," 150, 159, fig. 24; Dillon, *Girls and Women*, 46–50, 58–60, see esp. fig. 2.5, p. 46.

90. Beard et al., *Religions of Rome*, 51–54.

Although rigorously debated, evidence suggests that parents and caregivers took intimate interest in their babies in the face of high infant mortality. From infancy, wet-nurses were frequently used, although some ancient sources make a point to emphasize a mother who breast fed.[91] As early as the Greek classical period, we have intimate depictions of upper class infants or toddlers using potty stools (*lasanae*). One depiction, on a vase, depicts an infant adjacent its mother; the child has its arms extended toward her, and she reciprocates the gesture, smiling warmly.[92] Neils and Oakley also share images of terracotta figurines of nurses caring for infants and toddlers, which date from the fourth through third century BCE.[93] The evidence of nicknames such as "Tatae" and "Mammae" for biological parents, nurses, or other caregivers among some Roman families further suggests the sense of intimacy between caregivers and children in the Hellenistic world.[94]

As they developed from what we might consider toddlers into early childhood, children were expected to take on a little responsibility and training. Among the Greeks, and later the Romans, sons might be placed under the charge of a male *paedagogus* whose task was, in part, to aid in molding their character.[95] And like their Jewish counterparts, children in the wider Hellenistic and Roman world probably began engaging in domestic work by this time, contributing economically to the household.[96]

Nevertheless, archaeologists have uncovered numerous types of toys, including dolls and rattles, games, and evidence thereof, that demonstrate that some Greco-Roman children were able to share experiences that

---

91. For example, one inscription from Rome, recorded in the *CIL*, reads: "To Gratia Alexandria, an outstanding exemplar of modesty. She even brought up her children with the milk of her own breasts" (VI, 19128 = ILS 8451; Gardner and Wiedemann, *Roman Household*, 105). Also see the rebuke of a new grandmother, who wanted a nurse-maid to spare her daughter from nursing, by her son-in-law as recorded by Aulus Gellius (*Noctes Atticae* 12.1). On wet-nursing in antiquity, see Bradley, "Wet-nursing at Rome," 201–29; also Bradley, *Discovering*, 13–36.

92. Another, on a *chous*, shows an infant holding a rattle or some sort of object (Neils and Oakley, *Coming of Age*, 240–41, CAT).

93. Neils and Oakley, *Coming of Age*, 227–29, CAT.

94. Bradley, *Discovering*, 76–102.

95. Bradley, *Discovering*, 37–75.

96. There is an exceptional picture of a woman teaching a young girl to cook in Niels and Oakley, *Coming of Age*, 112, CAT. 61. It is a terracotta figurine from early fifth-century Greece.

we more often associate with childhood today, i.e., experiences of play.[97] The Roman rhetorician Quintilian approved of children's play, so long as it was not excessive. He mentions the deliberate integration of play with education in grammar.[98] Yet, we are probably safe to assume, not without evidence, that at some relatively early age the lives of non-elite children began to contrast sharply with the lives of elite children. Sometimes young children labored in apprenticeships under adverse conditions, as this brief letter from a child to his mother and one named Xenocles, a very rare find discovered in a well in the Athenian *agora*, indicates: "I have been handed over to a man thoroughly wicked; I am perishing from being whipped; I am tied up; I am treated like dirt—more and more!"[99] Meanwhile, education, whether in the form of apprenticeships, or grammar school and beyond, was increasingly widespread in the Hellenistic world, even among girls and slaves. Except for the presence of servants, for most of us, the descriptions of a young boy's typical school day from the third century CE sound eerily modern, even if idealized.

> Early in the morning, when I had woken up, I got up and I called the slave. I told him to open the window. He opened it quickly. When I had got up I sat down on the side of the bed. I called for my shoes and socks, because it was cold (HS).

97. Golden, *Children and Childhood*, 51–56. Here, Golden also emphasizes the linguistic connection between παῖς (child), παίζω (I play), and others sharing the same root. See also images of children at play, as well as ancient dolls discovered in Neils and Oakley, *Coming of Age*, 263–82, CAT. 67–94. For play among Roman children, see Wiedemann, *Adults and Children*, 146–153. It is impossible to say that non-elite or slave children never experienced some similar period of play, especially when very young. Rawson states that for Roman society: "In practice . . . children seem to have played freely in early childhood with a wide range of toys. Rome provided many occasions for gift-giving and many of the gifts given to children would have been toys. The Saturnalia festival provided great opportunities for this. Dolls were the most popular in a large range of toys, and there must have been an active toy-making industry, catering to all economic levels" (Rawson, "Adult-Child Relationships," 19–20).

98. "I quite approve . . . of a practice which has been devised to stimulate children to learn by giving them ivory letters to play with, as I do of anything else that may be discovered to delight the very young, the sight, handling and naming of which is a pleasure" (*Inst. Or.* 1.1.26; LCL). "There are moreover certain games which have an educational value for boys, as for instance when they compete in posing each other with all kinds of questions which they ask in turn and turn about" (*Inst. Or.* 1.3.11).

99. This inscription is on a lead tablet discovered in 1972. The quote is from Golden, "Childhood," 14. Golden cites Jordan, "A Personal Letter," 91–103. The preservation of thirty apprenticeship contracts for young boys in Roman Egypt attest that many children were often sent to learn a trade (Bradley, *Discovering*, 106–12).

[After dressing], I went out of the bedroom with the paedagogus and with the nurse to greet my father and mother. I greeted them both and I was kissed (CM).

Then I looked for my stylus and my notebook, and these I handed to my slave. With everything ready, I went out with a good omen and followed by my paedagogus went straight through the door which leads to school (HS).

I went in and I said "Greetings, sir." He kissed me and returned my greeting. My slave gave me my box of writing tablets, my case of styli, and my ruler. When I have sat down I smooth out my place [on the writing tablet] (CM).

I do my writing beside the examples to copy. When I have written, I show my work to the teacher. He corrects it and erases it. He orders me to read (CM).

When we have done these things, the teacher lets us go for lunch. Leaving school, I go home. I change, and I have white bread, olives, cheese, dried figs and nuts. I drink some cold water. When I have eaten I return again to school. I find the teacher reading out, and he said: "Begin from the beginning" (CM).[100]

In addition to biological children of parents, there sometimes lived non-biological children that played, worked, and died under the auspices

---

100. The passages, from the *Hermeneumata Stephani* and the *Colloquia Monacensia*, are juxtaposed together to give this impression of a full day in Strange, *Children*, 28. They represent, however, models of a proper school boy's behavior, and are written by an adult, who probably projects some of his own childhood into the accounts. On education of young girls, see Martial, *Epigrams* 9.68; Juvenal, *Satirae* 14.20–29; and frustration over women's education in Menander, *Fragment* 702K. The education of slaves is mentioned in Varro, *Rerum rusticarum* 1.17.4, and Pliny, *Epistulae* 5.19; 8.1.M. In addition to basic education or training in some craft, moral education and discipline were fundamental. It is generally believed that corporeal punishment was the norm in early childhood, and there was a strikingly modern form of debate over its merit among Roman sources. However, in a compelling chapter on the very subject, Richard Saller argues that Roman fathers reserved *uerbera* (corporeal punishment) for slaves and subjects rather than their own children (adolescent and above), despite their authority of *patria potestas*. For Romans, the point of whipping was not to instill pain for punishment, but humiliation, and citizens generally did not want to subject their children to the same form of humiliation as the servile class. Saller, "Corporeal Punishment," 144–65. On the shaping of versus the emergence of a child's moral character, see Dixon, *Roman Family*, 117–19.

of a Greek *kyrios* or Roman *paterfamilias*, who may have been a master, a patron, or, to borrow Rawson's terminology, a "foster-parent."[101] Romans appear to have distinguished between slave children purchased by a master and *vernae*, i.e., slave children born within the household. *Vernae* were generally treated better by their masters than non-*vernae* slaves.[102] *Alumnus* was a term peculiar to non-biological children of a special relational quality with caregivers in the Roman world.[103] Several legal passages and tomb inscriptions suggest or refer to parental affection toward *alumni*.[104] In some ways, Rawson believes they were socially similar to that of illegitimate children.[105] They were incorporated within a family, and also included in estate planning. On the other hand, some of the most disturbing accounts from Roman social history are tomb inscriptions, historical accounts, and satirical works that describe young slave boys or girls kept and affectionately referred to as a "pets" (*deliciae*) by some of the more wealthy citizens. They served as a source of constant amusement and joy.[106] However, these "historical" descriptions of *deliciae* are more likely acerbic critiques of the Roman imperial class as much as historical accounts, and like political attack ads today, their veracity may often be questionable.[107]

101. Rawson, "Children," 170–200.

102. Rawson's analyses of Roman children show that some *vernae* were granted their freedom and even incorporated into their former master's will, inheriting estates and carrying on their master's family *nomen* (ibid., 186–95); Dixon, *Roman Family*, 128.

103. Dixon defines them as foundlings raised, slave or free, as foster children within the family. Rawson suggests that, in addition to other factors, *alumni* carried an age connotation. Beyond some age in early adulthood, the description ceased to be used as a social signifier. Legal and inscriptional evidence all seem to suggest that the term always referred to dependents and minors (Rawson, "Children," 180–81, also on their status as slave or free).

104. See *CIL* VI, 31665 (Rome), cited in Gardner and Wiedemann, *Roman Household*, 42.

105. Rawson, "Children," 174–75. On pages 178–79, she also notes the discussion among historians over whether some *alumni* may have been illegitimate children.

106. Dio Cassius, *Hist. rom.* 48, 44.3; Herodian, *Hist.* 1.17.3; Martial, *Epigrams* 6.28–29. Compare his account with that of Dio Cassius' account of the naked boy Domitian kept (*Hist. rom.* 67.15.3).

107. Much of the past scholarship on *deliciae* has been driven by the seemingly pederastic relationship. More recently, Arthur Pomeroy has challenged the assertion that most of these "pets" were partly sexual playmates, in particular by deconstructing previous readings of Petronius's descriptions of the character Trimalchio in *Satyr.* 74.8; 75.11. Among others, Pomeroy challenges the reading of Bodel, "Trimalchio's Coming of Age," 72–74, and "Trimalchio and the Candelabrum," 224–31 (Pomeroy, "Trimalchio

Finally, simply in terms of affection and concern for children, there is much better attestation among Greco-Roman sources than from Jewish sources. Remember, however, here we are aided by the additions of artistic representations and a greater variety of literary genre. Furthermore, a paucity of comparable Jewish evidence does not necessarily imply a phenomenon did not exist. Of course, some scholars have charged that Greeks and Romans were largely indifferent about children, particularly the very young.

Xenophon asserts women have a greater affection for newborns over their husbands (*Oec* 7.24), and many sources describe parental love as a natural sentiment.[108] In *De providentia*, Seneca, the Stoic philosopher and tutor of the mid first century CE, describes the different displays of love shone a child between father and mother (*Dialogi* 2.5). Cicero suggests that love unites children and parents (*Fam.* 25.88). Balla includes a section in his monograph on the child-parent relationship on the prescriptive duty of children to love their parents among Greco-Roman writers.[109] And Pliny shows that affections from childhood may carry into adulthood, even for one's nurse, as he provided a generous provision for her in her old age (*Epistulae* 6.3).[110] There are, in addition, numerous images and epigraphic evidence suggestive of affections between caregivers and children from classical antiquity.[111]

In summary, children in Greek and Latin sources also existed in a wide array of conditions. As infants and toddlers they were raised under the watchful eyes of women and slaves until they could assume simple household tasks. Many boys and some girls received at least a grammar education and moral training. Religious worship, duties, and festivals were important parts of childhood education and social development within the family and community. Perhaps due in part to the prevalence of female deities and

---

as *Deliciae*," 45–53).

108. See Epictetus, *Diatr.* 1.16.3, 1.23.3–5; Plutarch, *Am. prol*; Cicero, *De oratore* 2.168; Cicero, *Att.* 7.2.4; Cicero, *De finibus* 3.62, 65; Cicero, *De officiis* 1.2; Cicero, *Epistulae ad familiares* 12.16.1; Pseudo-Dionysius of Halicarnassus, *Ars rhetorica* 2.3; Diogenes Laertius, *De clarorum philosophorum uitis* 7.120. For a contrary and utilitarian perception of children see Epicurus.

109. Balla, *Child-Parent Relationship*, 68–70.

110. On the issue of *patria potestas* and its relation to "love" or "affection," see Eyben, "Fathers and Sons," 115; also Saller, "Corporeal Punishment," 144–65.

111. For instance, Neils and Oakley, *Coming of Age;* and Gardner and Wiedemann, *Roman Household.*

sanctuaries devoted to them, and also to gods that made a special place for women devotees, such as Bacchus, it could even be argued that girls in these sources were able to experience a much richer religious experience than Jewish girls.[112] Children in the Hellenistic and Roman world were also segregated into gender-appropriate tasks as they grew. Nevertheless, whether orphaned, slave or free, boy or girl, *children were almost always dependent upon, and situated within a structured family setting,* whether a narrowly defined conjugal unit of father, mother, and child, or a much broader household structure that encompassed step-parent, foster-parent, a master over an apprentice, or child-minders.

Conclusion

Could children act as autonomous characters, independent of the authority of caretakers? In other words, did children have agency? Could they have left home and family, as the children of Cologne reportedly did? Apparently nothing of the sort was possible in the Jewish context. Suspending examination of the gospel literature until the next chapter, I have found no evidence among Jewish sources from the period of roughly 300 BCE-200 CE that presents a child or children acting autonomously from their caregivers.

Furthermore, among our Greek and Latin sources of the period, again, our answer appears to be no, not in its most literal sense anyway. The closest examples in this literature are: 1) the presence of children among initiates to the Eleusinian or Bacchian mysteries, or when children left home for religious consecration and a set period of service to a particular temple; 2) the prolonged apprenticeships that kept children away from home, learning a particular trade or craft. As has already been mentioned, boys and girls were often consecrated for a period of service in a temple.

In terms of affection or concern for children *as children*, it seems there is ample Greek and Latin evidence to offset suggestions that Jesus' concern for young children, as portrayed in the Synoptic gospels, was unique or extraordinary for the period. Despite a paucity of such evidence for Jewish culture at large, I suspect affections and concern were not measurably

112. If Lev 15 is understood as Exilic or Post-exilic literature, then Wegner has demonstrated that within the earliest Priestly circles of Second-Temple Judaism, women were spatially excluded from bringing sacrifices *before the Lord*. It was done on their behalf (Wegner, "Coming Before the Lord," 451–65). Pushing her thesis further, I have argued that women were excluded as recipients of divine speech in Leviticus. God speaks to Moses, who in turn addresses only Israelite men directly. Murphy, "Ignoring Women."

different for Jewish caregivers and the children thereof. On the whole, most children were welcomed, integral members of familial life at various levels. Absolutely vulnerable otherwise, they were entirely dependent on structured family settings for food, shelter, and protection.

CHAPTER THREE

THE KINGDOM, DISCIPLESHIP, AND FAMILY TIES IN THE SYNOPTIC GOSPELS

> Jesus loves the little children, all the children of the world.
> Red and yellow, black and white,
> They are precious in his sight.
> Jesus loves the little children of the world.[1]

BY OUTLINING SOME OF the *realia* of late ancient Jewish and Hellenistic-Roman family life in chapter two, I have shown that children in Hellenistic-Roman and Jewish worlds were in fact quite dependent on adult caregivers, not acting autonomously. Furthermore, neither Jesus nor the Synoptic authors were unique in expressions of affection and concern for children as children. Now, we are poised to explore the links between children, discipleship, and the kingdom of God. First, how do the authors situate children in relation to the kingdom and discipleship? Better yet, how do they *convince us* of such links? Are there clues to the artificiality of their narrative world? Second, if children were so thoroughly situated within the care of adult caregivers, often some family setting, how does the Jesus of the Synoptics solicit children and their families to make disciples, or kingdom members, of them?

In order to accomplish these goals, first, I shall examine passages where Jesus interacts with, or comments about, non-adult children. This involves analyzing ways in which the Synoptic authors construct their narratives, foregrounding children in order to emphasize not only the socially inclusive nature of the eschatological kingdom, but to highlight exemplary

1. Lyrics by C. Herbert Woolston (1856–1927), public domain.

characteristics of kingdom membership. In the process, I shall show how scholars, particularly (but not limited to) child-theologians, have interpreted passages referencing children.

I begin with the three healing narratives shared among the Synoptics, in which child characters play a pivotal role in furthering the plot, signaling the apocalypse of the kingdom of God: 1) Jairus' daughter (Mark 5:21–24, 35–43; Matt 9:18–19, 23–26; Luke 8:40–42, 49–56); 2) the Syrophoenician/Canaanite woman's daughter (Mark 7:24–30; Matt 15:21–28); and 3) a boy with a demon (Mark 9:14–27; Matt 17:14–18; Luke 9:37–43). These healings are enormously significant for the study of children, for the Synoptic authors seemingly depict Jesus' concern for them as individuals worthy of attention. This portion of my examination of Synoptic portrayals of children will culminate with two pericopae that have most often been used to emphasize Jesus' inclusivity toward children: the "Child in the Midst" (Mark 9:33–36; Matt 18:1–5; 10:40; Luke 9:46–48) and "Let the Little Children Come to Me" (Mark 10:13–16; Matt 19:13–15; Luke 18:15–17).

Second, since children have been shown to be wholly dependent on some form of adult supervision for this period, I shall summarize the problematic relationship between the Synoptic authors' portrayal of Jesus' eschatological gathering of followers and traditional familial structures, using Gerd Theissen's concept of "itinerant charismatics," as well as Barton's articulation of the problematic relationship between discipleship and family structures.

Let me say at the outset that, like several recent child-theologians, I believe the Synoptic authors deliberately attempt to include children in their narratives, and to convey that they are included among Jesus' new fictive family.

Although my analysis is ultimately a literary interpretation, I want to know whether we can "buy into" the authors' characterization of children, based upon what we know historically about children, traditional family structures in Jewish antiquity, and reconstructions of the Jesus movement. In conjunction with this approach, my interpretive reading will assume a particular sociological reconstruction of the Jesus movement, based on the Synoptic Gospels. First, however, I shall examine how the Synoptic authors set out to convince us that Jesus and his band of eschatological followers were inclusive of children.

Attempting Child Inclusivity by the Synoptic Authors

In chapter two, I showed that there is a rich diversity of references to children in Hellenistic and Roman art and literature, some quite sentimental, others reinforce their marginal status in society. Similarly, Jewish evidence, although a much smaller body of entirely literary sources, shows that their own children were generally important to Jewish culture and theology, yet they remained very marginal figures in society. Although children might frequently spend significant time away from parents or primary caregivers, as apprentices, as slaves that may have been separated from them by sale, or during periods of consecration and service to the gods at local temples, they seem to have always been dependent upon an adult. Furthermore, when they did leave their family in one of these capacities, they did so because of the actions or directive of their primary caregiver, which most typically was their father or master.

With this in mind, we must examine the Synoptic Gospels in order to determine whether their depictions of children comport with the findings of chapter two. How do the Synoptic authors portray children in relation to discipleship, the kingdom, and to Jesus? Can they act autonomous of adults toward Jesus? Are Synoptic portrayals of children realistic or plausible? If commentators and ministers find them convincing, why?

In general, the Synoptic authors depict a radically inclusive kingdom in which Jesus reaches out especially to marginal figures such as women, Gentiles, the sick, the poor, and ritually impure. And although Jesus is depicted as a teacher, action seems even more characteristic of this main character. He moves from town to town, from desert to villages, to city. He heals, casts out demons, and performs miraculous events. He calls many to himself, and several passages attest various "disciples" following him, while occasionally "the crowd" follows him.[2] And while children do appear fre-

---

2. In Mark, this includes not only the calling of Simon and Andrew (1:16–18) and James and John (1:19–20), but those whom he called to himself (προσκαλεῖται, 3:13) and made apostles, the Twelve whom he called to commission for teaching and healing around Galilee (6:7), and the disciples or the twelve whom he called to himself to discuss the demands of discipleship on at least four other occasions (8:34, 9:35, 10:42, and 12:43). Yet he called to or for the crowd at 7:14 and again at 8:34, the latter with the disciples in order to explain to all of them the cost of following him. From the crowd Jesus called Levi (2:13–15) and Bartimaeus (10:48), whose sight he restored; both followed him (Malbon, *Company of Jesus*, 72–75). Interestingly, in her narrative reading of Mark, Malbon refers to both of these groups, the "disciples," properly so-called, and the crowd, as "fallible followers" (41–99).

quently in the Synoptic narratives, they are easily overlooked. Why? First, we are typically more interested in the protagonist. Second, real children were considered socially marginal.[3] Third, children are depicted solely as minor characters, meaning there are no recurring child characters.[4] Like an ember that emerges from a campfire in the night, they flicker in a singular glow and are quickly extinguished. So it is with intent that we look specifically for child characters as we read, approaching the narrative foremost for them, and relegating the other characters to the margins.

Since the concern of this project is with the intersection of children and the Jesus movement, discussions of certain child characters will be left to a later date: e.g., the infants John and Jesus in Matthew and Luke's infancy narratives, and the dancing daughter of Herodias.[5] As for our movement through the texts, I assume Markan priority and will loosely follow his arrangement of the pertinent texts, examining the parallel treatments as we go. There are also a number of passages in Matthew and Luke not found in Mark. Some are more important to this study than others and will be treated where they bear most upon my thesis. Among scholars, most attention has been given to the pericopae of the "Child in the Midst" and "Let the Young Children Come to Me." Therefore, these passages will be the objects of greatest emphasis in this study.

Restoring Children to their Caregivers: The Healing Narratives

Among the Synoptics, children are first prominently portrayed during Jesus' ministry in a series of three healing narratives, where parents or caregivers entreat Jesus on their behalf for healing: Jairus' daughter (Mark 5:21–24, 35–43 and par.), the Syrophoenician/Canaanite woman's daughter (Mark 7:24–30 and par.), and a boy with a demon (Mark 9:14–27 and par.).

Mark leads us to the first of these healings in staccato-like movement. Jesus is immediately busy; Mark overwhelms the reader with his presence, what he teaches is punctuated by what he does and his quick movements.

---

3. For a social-scientific commentary on the status of children in antiquity, see Malina and Rohrbaugh, *Social-Scientific Commentary*, 238.

4. Malbon shows how this is true for Mark (*Company of Jesus*, 192).

5. Despite my singular focus on the role of children during Jesus' adult life, I find Sharon Betsworth's recent argument that Matthew intends 18:1–5 to be read through the prism of the infancy narrative in Matthew 2 quite convincing. Contra White, she writes: "While it is true that Jesus does not make the connection, Matthew certainly does" (Betsworth, "Child and Jesus," 10n24). Cf. White, "He Placed a Little Child," 258–59.

He teaches, heals, and casts out demons all over Galilee, gathering a host of followers. By the middle of chapter five, a young girl and only child (κοράσιον; Mark 5:41, 42; Matt 9:24, 25) lies at her life's end under her desperate parents' care (Mark 5:21–23 and par.).[6] Questions come to mind. Is she awake when we are first introduced to her? Is she crying for her parents? Does she care for them as much as we intuit, through the actions of her father, that they care for her?

It is her father, called Jairus in Mark and Luke, who carries the narrative. He is a religious leader, one who should have God on speed dial about such matters. He has heard about Jesus, one of those "holy" men that appear from time to time, who reportedly are able to restore the sick. He goes to Jesus and, prostrate, pleads with him to come "lay your hands on her, so that she may be made well (σώζω),[7] and live" (Mark 5:23). The girl dies, only Jesus insists she is sleeping (Mark 5:39 par.). Yet the father seems to be the character most in focus, especially when Jesus tells him, μὴ φοβοῦ, μόνον πίστευε (omitted by Matthew). When he arrives in the house, he takes her hand and tells her to get up (Mark 5:41; Luke 8:54).[8] The last thing Mark tells us about her is that she gets up, walks about, and that Jesus tells them to give her some food (vv. 42–43). This only child is restored to her parents and they are amazed (Mark 5:42; Luke 8:56).

The Synoptics seem to portray Jesus just as concerned for this young girl as the older people whom he has healed or exorcised. He goes to her rather than having her brought to him; he takes hold of her hand and speaks

---

6. In Matthew, Jesus calls his disciples, goes throughout Galilee appearing in synagogues, proclaiming his kingdom message, healing the sick, and gathering crowds from Galilee, Syria, "the Decapolis, Jerusalem, Judea," and the Transjordan (4:18–25). Then Jesus delivers the first of five Matthean discourses (5:1–7:27) from a hillside. Matthew sets the healing of the synagogue leader's daughter within his first collection of miracle stories (8:1–9:34) She is already dead when her father reaches Jesus. Luke depicts Jesus teaching and healing throughout Galilee (4:14–15) and Judea (4:44). He delivers his "sermon on the plain" (6:17–49) and increasingly is involved with the most marginal of society in a series of healings, exorcisms, and teachings before commissioning the Twelve in chapter nine. Luke situates the account of Jairus' daughter at the end of this material in chapter eight.

7. This term can also be translated "save her from the end" or "rescue from harm" (LS, "σώζω," 687).

8. Matthew has Jesus take her hand and she gets up without him addressing her (9:25).

directly to her; he then displays concern that she is given food to sustain and strengthen her.[9]

After taking us on a tour of lower Galilee and the lake region again, Mark and Matthew lead us to the region of Tyre. There, a Syrophoenician woman, whose θυγάτριον is reportedly possessed by a demon, heard that a healer has come into town (Mark 7:25; Matt 15:22).[10] Again, the young girl appears to be an only child and is nameless; she is not introduced, nor does she come to Jesus. We are only told she is home in bed (7:30). If she is fatherless, the two are perhaps almost destitute (at least they still have a home). The poor mother has had to somehow economically support herself and her daughter through her own efforts and whatever charity she can glean.[11] Her daughter is of little help, but the circumstances surrounding their plight seem inconsequential.[12] The authors are more concerned with Jesus' verbal exchange with the mother. She begs him to cast out the demon and Jesus likens her and her daughter to "dogs" in his response (Mark 7:27; Matt 15:26). The "children of Israel" come first, not heathens, much less their children. Yet, because the woman shamelessly bared her humility and acknowledged her reliance on the mercy of any healer that could help, the demon was cast out.

Finally, in Mark 9:14–29 (Matt 17:14–21; Luke 9:37–43a) we are introduced to a παιδίον who struggles under the possession of a demon.[13] He

9. Luke repeats as much, but Matthew omits the directive to her parents and their reaction to the resurrection.

10. Matthew designates the woman a "Χαναναία" (Canaanite; 15:22). After healing the synagogue leader's daughter, Matthew's Jesus itinerates throughout Galilee (9:35–37). He commissions the Twelve to itinerate throughout Galilee and tells them what to expect (chapter ten). In 11:1 he seems to separate from the disciples and begins itinerating again alone throughout Galilee. He reproaches the lake towns for their unbelief, gives various teachings in 12:1–45, has an altercation with his biological family, clarifying his "true kindred" (12:46–50), and begins a short series of miracles again in chapters fourteen and fifteen. After feeding the five thousand (14:13–21), the Matthean Jesus leaves Gennesaret for the region of Sidon and Tyre (14:34; 15:21). Matthew sandwiches the exorcism of the Canaanite woman's daughter between two feeding miracles. Luke does not include a parallel account of this healing.

11. But see Betsworth, who suggests they may have been well off (*Reign of God*, 129–30, esp. n102).

12. The girl's father is never mentioned. In Matthew, the disciples tell Jesus to "ἀπόλυσον αὐτήν" (15:23).

13. Matthew and Luke follow Mark's placement of the pericope directly after the Transfiguration. Following Mark, Luke says the boy is possessed by a πνεῦμα. Matthew initially does not refer to possession and instead uses the term σεληνιάζεται—to be

suffers from uncontrollable epileptic-like convulsions in which his mouth foams and he tenses up. When it affects the boy, he falls to the ground wherever he is, whether near the hearth, the tanner's fire, or the streambed. One can envision the boy bruised and battered, scarred by burn marks. He is a drain on his father's resources, unable to contribute to the household or become a future caretaker for his father. Mark alone says this is not a sudden affliction; the poor boy has been like this since παιδιόθεν, "childhood" (9:21). In his account, years of suffering have elapsed for this child.

The boy's father has been concerned, perhaps has sought help for years. A holy man or prophet and his disciples happen through, and the father seizes his son and gets him to the healers. Much to their credit, the disciples try to cast out the demon, yet they are unsuccessful (Mark 9:18 and par.). This time, Jesus is confronted with the child. He sees him convulsing. Then, he casts out the spirit that had seized him, in turn seizes the hand of the boy, who lay "like a corpse," and raises him up (Mark 9:25–27).[14]

Taken together, these healings and exorcisms underscore not just the inclusion of Gentiles but, for many interpreters, the Synoptic authors' (or Jesus') concerns for children, and their inclusion in the kingdom of God. In her study of daughters in Mark, Sharon Betsworth asserts that it is the minor characters, including children, who illustrate how to become and remain faithful when others do not. They are those "who appear briefly, respond positively to Jesus, and then slip away never to be seen again."[15] For example, she notes that σώζειν (to save) is used frequently in Mark for those healed from sickness or death, but also refers to eschatological notions of eternal life and the reign of God; i.e., "Healing . . . and being saved . . . are nearly one and the same" in Mark.[16] In the healing and exorcism narratives, typically someone hears Jesus and responds positively on behalf of themselves, a son, or daughter; and so for Betsworth, "All people who have faith, Jews and Greeks, who hear and respond, are a part of the Reign of God."[17] Meanwhile, Gundry concludes that these "miracles for children imply that children are those for whom the kingdom of God has drawn near; they

"moon-struck" or a "lunatic"; 17:15 (LS, "σεληνιάζομαι," 632). However, in 17:18 he tells us that Jesus cast a δαιμόνιον from him.

14. Matthew and Luke omit several details here, reporting only that Jesus rebuked the spirit, immediately healing the boy (Matt 17:18; Luke 9:42), and Luke adds that he was restored to his father.

15. Betsworth, *Reign of God*, 100.

16. Ibid., 100–101.

17. Ibid., 134.

are among its intended beneficiaries."[18] This interpretation is clearly built on the proviso that the temporal kingdom of God becomes manifested in the Synoptics through Jesus' actions (teachings, healings, miracles), and the socially marginal, largely minor characters, who hear and respond or are "saved," including children, are disproportionately counted as members.[19] For the most part, I think this is a fairly solid and very assuring interpretation, one of which the Synoptic authors want to convince us.

Moreover, Betsworth argues that the figure of Jesus, the Son of God, functions as a "divine guardian and protector" of females, although one could probably substitute "children" or "socially marginal" for "females." In support, she compares the divine care and affection of Jesus for females in Mark to the divine care and affection for young females by gods and goddesses in several Greek and Jewish works from antiquity. In doing so, she also supports one of my contentions, that is, that the depictions of the Synoptic authors of divine care and affection for children by Jesus was not all that unique in ancient literature.[20]

Kids and the Kingdom: the Inclusion of Children According to Jesus

The significance of children for the Synoptics culminates with two pericopae that foreground children in their respective conceptions of the kingdom and discipleship.[21] At first appearances, this literary move, at least rhetorically, places children on social par with all others. I shall refer to the first pericope as the "Child in the Midst."

For most commentators, this pericope, and the one to follow, are interpreted against the Synoptic theme of great social reversal intrinsic to the kingdom of God. And for Jesus and his encroaching kingdom (i.e., the Synoptic authors' portrayals of it), children and some quality/ies about them are centrally important. Their characterization contrasts sharply with their

---

18. Gundry, "Children," 151.

19. Betsworth, *Reign of God*, 135.

20. Ibid., 60–95.

21. The phrase in Mark 9:42 and parallels, "one of these little ones," is frequently taken to reference children, but not without challenge. The more explicit ambiguity of this phrase and its various contexts lends its entire discussion to the deconstructive reading in chapter 4.

marginal status in antiquity.[22] Therefore, it is argued, the Synoptic authors' depiction of a child, Jesus actions toward children, the spatial arrangement of characters, the preserved sayings tradition, and several other interpretive devices function to demonstrate the *inclusiveness* of the kingdom of God.[23]

After the Markan accounts of the Transfiguration (9:2ff) and the exorcism of the possessed boy (9:14–29), Jesus and his followers attempt to pass stealthily through Galilee once more, toward Capernaum. On the way, he forewarns the disciples of his imminent pouring out of self in suffering and death (9:30), only to be confronted with their self-interest in deciding which among them is most important for the kingdom.

> And they came to Capernaum. And being in the house he asked them, "What were you arguing about on the way?" But they remained silent, for on the way they had debated with one another over who was greatest. And he sat down and called the Twelve and said to them, "If anyone wants to be first, he must be last of all and a servant to all."[24] And taking a young child (λαβὼν παιδίον) he placed it in their midst and taking it into his arms (ἐναγκαλισάμενος), he said to them, "Whoever welcomes one of such young children (ἓν τῶν τοιούτων παιδίων)[25]in my name, welcomes me; and whoever welcomes me, does not welcome me but the one who sent me." (Mark 9:33–37)

> And an argument arose among them as to who might be greatest. But Jesus, knowing[26] the content of their hearts, taking a young child (ἐπιλαβόμενος παιδίον[27]), he placed him next to himself and said to them, "Whoever welcomes this young child (τοῦτο τὸ

22. For example, Perkins writes that "to insist that receiving a child might have some value for male discipleship is almost inconceivable" (Perkins, *Mark*, 637). Likewise, Crossan uses similar terminology, stating in his monumental work, *Historical Jesus*, 269: "But what would ordinary Galilean peasants have thought about children? . . . a kingdom of children is a kingdom of nobodies"; Gundry disputes Crossan's characterization based on her reading of children in Jewish history (Gundry, "Children," 162).

23. Cf. Perkins, *Mark*, 647.

24. The following ancient Markan manuscripts omit this sentence: D k.

25. In Mark, ℵ C Δ (Ψ) *pc* substitute τοιούτων παιδίων (such children) with παιδίων τούτων (these children).

26. εἰδὼς—here, several substantial Lukan witnesses attest the word "seeing" [ἰδων], including A C D L W Θ Ξ Ψ 0115 $f^{1.13}$ 33 and *Majority Text*. However, NA[27] and the UBSGNT 4th Edition chose the present "knowing" attested in ℵ B K 700. 1424. 2542 *al.*

27. Here in Luke, NA[27] notes that ℵ A L W Θ Ξ Ψ 0115 $f^{1.13}$ 33 and *Majority Text* attest the genitive form παιδίου.

παιδίον) in my name welcomes me; and [whoever welcomes me welcomes][28] the one who sent me. For the least among all of you is the greatest." (Luke 9:46–48)

For our study, it seems significant that Jesus and his disciples were in a house (v.33; only in Mark). The setting intimately ties them to notions of family, so it is not surprising that a young child (παιδίον) is nearby. After the question of greatness is raised, Mark sets the interpretive tone for his account by stating that anyone wanting to be great, in the kingdom, must be "last of all and servant of all" (9:35). Acts of service to others, or the status of servanthood, are then linked with the child in verse 36 by use of paronomasia, where παιδίον can mean "young child," "slave," or "child slave."[29] In other words, Mark's overall point is about social rank.[30] In order to enter the kingdom, one must become a servant, even to the likes of children.[31]

In response to his disciples' discussion, Mark and Matthew tell us that Jesus took a child and set it in their midst (Mark 9:36 and par), an act that should be nothing short of astounding for the Synoptic authors to convey. For as Keith White points out, all sorts of people "unclean, poor, beggars, Gentiles, women, and sinners," came to Jesus. "However, at no point does Jesus choose one of these as a sign of the kingdom of heaven by placing them in the midst of the disciples."[32] Significantly, the Matthean Jesus *calls* the child to him (προσκαλεω), echoing the calling of disciples in Matt 10:1, and is therefore associated with the kingdom and discipleship.[33] Who is this child? It is probably a young boy, since Mark makes it clear elsewhere

---

28. In Luke, this phrase is omitted in Codex Bezae.

29. Marcus, *Mark 8–16*, 681. Strange asserts that children entered the kingdom of God based on "their objective position in society which made them models of discipleship," not on their "subjective characteristics." And because the Aramaic word for "child" also translated as "servant," Jesus "*meant*" that entering the kingdom as a child is to enter a life of "service and humility." However, Strange asks a question fundamental to this study: Did Jesus mean it belongs to those who become humble *like children*, but not to children themselves? For Strange, Jesus' action in this pericope suggests that children were important *in the kingdom* (Strange, *Children*, 51; my emphasis).

30. Müller writes: "Das Kind als Gegenbild zum Rangstreben der Jünger wird damit zugleich zum *beispiel* für alle, die wie die Kinder 'gering' sind" (Müller, *In der Mitte*, 220); also see Liebenberg, *Language*, 471n124; Myers, "As a Child," 18.

31. This is the literal rendering which Gundry arrives at through the Markan account: "Thus, to be great in the reign of God, disciples have *to love and serve children*" ("Least and the Greatest," 42; "To Such as These," 475; my emphasis).

32. White, "He Placed a Little Child," 353–54.

33. Carter, *Households and Discipleship*, 96.

when the character is a young girl. Yet the potential ambiguity permits a young modern reader to identify him or herself with the child. Was this child within the same room as the group, listening to the unfolding discussion, or in an adjacent room? Were there siblings present? For the Synoptic authors, all such questions seem superfluous. All that matters for a brief moment is that *a child* is taken by Jesus and placed in a central position within the narratives. The spatial proximity of the child is significant for the authors. Despite the often clueless nature of the Twelve in Mark, it seems logical that they are either already counted as kingdom insiders (e.g., Mark 3:31–35) or foremost candidates for entry. Commenting on Matthew's text, Eugene Boring believes the disciples had "presumed" they were already kingdom people.[34] Yet here, the child is in the middle with Jesus; the Twelve and any other disciples present are, momentarily at least, one concentric step away from them looking inward. With subtle difference of style, Luke places the child *next to* Jesus (9:47), emphasizing the socially leveling aspect of the kingdom, or the great social reversal where the least becomes the greatest.[35]

Then, as if to drive home the point of Jesus' concern for children *qua children*, Mark has Jesus take the child up in his arms, or embrace him (ἐναγκαλισάμενος).[36] Matthew and Luke omit the embrace. Joel Marcus notes that the use of λαβον ("to take, seize, take hold of") and ἐναγκαλισάμενος ("embracing") in Mark 9:36 may imply a symbolic adoption in some venues.[37] In his book *Children in the Early Church*, William A. Strange refers to Jesus "embrace" here and in 10:16 as a "cuddle," which "symbolized his protection and care."[38]

Suddenly the interpreter recognizes that the Synoptic authors have done nothing short of bringing children out the shadows of social marginality in the "real" world and situate them in a place of distinction in

---

34. Boring, *Matthew*, 374; cf. White, "He Placed a Little Child," 364.

35. Kodell shares an intriguing comment on the parallel texts at this point. "When Jesus takes the child into the midst of the disciples, an earth tremor seems to pass through the threefold Synoptic narrative. Mark's narrative is suddenly disorganized and unfocused, and both Matthew and Luke separate from his story line after a few verses in order to incorporate material from Q and from their special sources. Up to this point, Matthew and Luke have been following Mark in the longest simultaneous parallel before the Judean section" (Kodell, "Luke and the Children," 420).

36. LS, "ἐναγκαλίζομαι," 221.

37. Marcus, *Mark*, 675.

38. Strange, *Children*, 49.

the kingdom of God. For most theological interpreters thus far who have actually devoted much attention to the child in the text, we can safely paraphrase: Is it not amazing how "Jesus loves the little children"; or, for some: how remarkable it is among the writers of antiquity for the Synoptic authors to treat children in such an inclusive manner. The kingdom of God engulfs the child. Still, I wonder as an interpreter, how does this child feel about the situation? Like my eight-year-old, would this child be embarrassed to be "put on the spot" before a group of adults? Does the child get it?—i.e., that he or she is included and socially important to the authors or their protagonist? Does the child recognize this person in the house, holding her, as a prophet or healer?[39] As Israel's messiah? A god? Or, does the child merely see a man using her to make a point to the other adults in the room? Does she recognize the apocalypse of the eschatological kingdom?[40]

Then the "walls come tumbling down." With this pericope, the Synoptic authors make explicit what some of Jesus' miracles have intuited thus far. The presence of children is a key indicator of the apocalypse of the kingdom of God. "Whoever welcomes one of such children in my name, welcomes me; and whoever welcomes me, does not welcome me but the one who sent me" (Mark 9:37; cf. Matt 18:5 and Luke 9:48). In this kingdom, a child is an ambassador, a representative of Jesus himself, and further, an ambassador of God.[41] John Carroll appropriately uses the word "hospitality," a characteristically Lukan theme.[42] This passage should recall for readers the sending out of the disciples in Mark 6:11 (Matt 10:14; Luke 9:5). They were vulnerable and dependent upon the hospitality of those who welcomed them.[43] Matthew changes "one of such children" to "one such child," while Luke concretizes the saying to read "this child." Luke, emphasizing that the

39. Use of the feminine here and subsequently merely reflects my own sense of inclusivity as the father of two young daughters. There is also an additional sense of compensation for girls which usually, in antiquity, were functionally treated as inferior to boys.

40. I use *apocalypse* in this phrase in its most literal sense to mean "unveiling" or "revelation."

41. Francis, "Children and Childhood," 73; Donahue and Harrington, *Mark*, 285.

42. Carroll, "What Then Will This Child Become?," 189. Gundry also points out that δεχομαι holds particular notions of hospitality. So to receive a child in Jesus' name suggests welcoming *and serving it*. "Thus, to be great in the reign of God, disciples have to love and serve children" (Gundry, "Least and the Greatest," 43; Gundry, "To Such as These," 475).

43. Myers draws out the contrast: now the disciples refuse to accept a child and the social transformation declared by Jesus in 9:35 (Myers, "As a Child," 18).

eschatological kingdom greatly upsets the social norms of this world, adds in superlative form that the "least among all of you is the greatest." The lowly become the greatest and the significant are brought low.[44]

The Matthean account is significantly different in a couple of ways. The first difference, that Matthew places this pericope much later in his text, providing substantially more narrative background, will be examined here. The second, Matthew's insertion of "little ones" into Mark's saying on giving "a cup of water" (Matt 10:42), and substantially forwarding this saying in the text, will be examined in chapter four.

> At that time the disciples came to Jesus saying, "Who is great-est in the kingdom of heaven?" And calling a young child (προσκαλεσάμενος παιδίον), he placed him in their midst and said, ["Truly I tell you, unless you change and become like young children, you will never enter the kingdom of heaven.][45] There-fore, whoever humbles him or herself like this young child (ὡς τὸ παιδίον τοῦτο); that one is the greatest in the kingdom of heaven. And whoever welcomes one such young child (ἓν παιδίον τοιοῦτο) in my name, welcomes me. (Matt 18:1–5) Whoever welcomes you welcomes me, and whoever welcomes me welcomes the one who sent me. (Matt 10:40)[46]

Matthew inserts references to children in several places along the Gal-ilean path of Jesus and his eschatological band. Some of it is shared tradi-tion with Luke (Q material), and some of it is his own doing. For the sake of brevity, these references will not receive full exegetical treatment. They are catalogued here, however, to support the contention that the Synoptic au-thors want readers to note the inclusion of non-adult children in their texts. As early as the "Sermon on the Mount," in Matt 7:9–11 (cf. Luke 11:11–13) Jesus assumes that caregivers know how to give good gifts to their τέκνον ("children"). In Matt 11:16–17 (Luke 7:31–32) the authors suggest their protagonist has some familiarity with childish taunts in a marketplace. However, it is of particular interest that Matthew alone tells us at the con-clusion of 14:21 that Jesus miraculously fed five thousand "besides women *and children*," and in 15:38 that he fed four thousand "besides women *and*

---

44. For Kodell, "lowliness" is the primary quality of discipleship in Luke ("Luke and the Children," 424–25), which translates to a status of "powerlessness" and complete "dependence on God" (429–30); cf. L. Johnson, *Luke*, 160; also Fitzmyer views the entire portion about Jesus and children in Luke as a teaching about humility (*Luke*, 816).

45. Matthew 8:3 actually parallels Mark 10:15 and Luke 18:17.

46. There are no significant textual variants in Matthew 18:1–5 or 10:40.

children" (παιδίων in both instances). For Matthew, children are not only the objects of miracles; they are also among the *hearers* of Jesus.

These inclusions bring us to the current pericope over children and the discussion of greatness in Matthew. After placing the child he had called into their midst, the Matthean Jesus adds:

> Truly I tell you, unless you change and become like young children, you will never enter the kingdom of heaven. Therefore, whoever humbles him or herself like this young child; that one is the greatest in the kingdom of heaven. (Matt 18:3–4)[47]

By including these verses, this child in Matthew may understand that he or she is being held up as an example to adults. She is more aligned with the kingdom of heaven than those currently surrounding her. For them, to get "in," they must become *like* this young child. Eugene Boring finds this act the Synoptic equivalent of John 3:3, 5—an act of conversion. Of the meanings attributed over time to "becoming like a little child," he lists: "humble, innocent, without lust, open and trusting, spontaneous, vulnerable and dependent," and "allowing oneself to be given a gift without a compulsion to 'deserve' it." However, Matthew is explicit that the child-like quality necessary to enter the kingdom is the status of humility.[48] Those

---

47. Verse three here roughly parallels Mark 10:15 and Luke 18:17.

48. Gundry, To Such as These," 474–75; "Least and Greatest," 41–42; Carter asserts regarding Matthew that "becoming as children" is explicated in 18:4 as "humbling oneself" (cf. Matt 11:29 where Jesus is described as the "humble one"). "This humbling is equated with believing in Jesus (18.6), the starting point of discipleship, and will result in being exalted at the final judgment (23:12), its goal" (*Households and Discipleship*, 96–97); Taylor-Wingender ("Kids of the Kingdom," 20) adds "vulnerability" to humility as the qualities of greatness Jesus saw in children. In the Anchor Bible commentary, Albright and Mann seem rather inattentive to the particulars of this passage and the characters therein. Regarding Matt 18:3, they simply state that the central concern is that "only those who know they cannot possibly *earn* God's grace . . . can fully respond to it," just as children know they cannot "earn free gifts" (Albright and Mann, *Matthew*, 216). Boring contends Matthew has retooled a Q expression used also in 23:12 (cf. Luke 14:11; 18:14) to mean to "humble oneself, giving up all pretensions of self-importance, independence, and self-reliance and turning in trust to the heavenly Father. The story is not a call to imitate the (presumed) character traits of children, but to accept a radically different understanding of status . . . abandon the quest for status and accept one's place as already given in the family of God" (*Matthew*, 374). The narrative reading of Betsworth is the most interesting thus far, who notes that Matthew portrays in chapter two a child that is "vulnerable, threatened with death, and completely dependent upon others, including God." Forward to 18:1–5, she writes: "As Jesus sets the child before [the disciples], he is setting before them the example of his own life. They are to be vulnerable has he was, threatened as he was, and to be reliant on God as he was. In short, his disciples are to

who take on the humble status of children will be greatest in Matthew's kingdom of heaven.

Having coming from Galilee into Judea and then beyond the Jordan, Mark again portrays Jesus teaching, when some Pharisees confront him over the Torah's bearing on divorce. Asserting that a couple becomes "one flesh" under God, Jesus then elaborates on the matter to the disciples "in the house" (10:10). Within Mark's narrative, this house is presumably somewhere east of the Jordan outside Judea. To whom the house belongs seems irrelevant. Nonetheless, the reference is probably not incidental to Mark, since in this section the author has juxtaposed teachings on marriage, children, and property, each a component of typical Hellenistic "Household Codes."[49]

After the teaching on remarriage, which seemingly highlights the importance of family, Mark then narrates:

> And they were bringing young children (παιδία) to him so that he might touch them. But the disciples denounced them.[50] But watching, Jesus became irate and said to them, "Let the young children (τὰ παιδία) come to me, do not hold them back, for the kingdom of God consists of such like these. Truly I tell you, whoever does not welcome the kingdom of God like a young child (ὡς παιδίον), will never enter it. And having taken them into his arms

---

become like the child he was and also like the vulnerable and threatened adult he will become. This is the humility they are to embody as his followers" (Betsworth, "Child and Jesus," 11, 13).

49. Aristotle, *Pol.* 1.1253b 7–8, 12–14; Osiek and Balch, *Families*, 119; deSilva, *Honor*, 178–92; Stambaugh and Balch, *New Testament in Its Social Environment*, 123–24; Jeffers, *Greco-Roman World*, 237–49. In Matthew, after Jesus finishes teaching on various temptations, on admonishing sinning members of the church, and on forgiveness, he leaves Galilee behind and heads into "Judea beyond the Jordan" (19:1). Matthew then follows the Markan household code format very closely: remarriage, children, and wealth (19:3–30). Carter argues that Matt 19–20 consists of an inverted (or subverted) form of the four typical subjects of household codes: husband over wife, father over children, master over slave, and the acquisition of wealth." Within this section, Carter views 19:13–15 as a natural continuation of narration when read against the background of household codes. Given this assessment, he characterizes the inclusion of 19:12 on eunuchs as a surprising interruption to modern readers (Carter, *Households and Discipleship*, 9, 90).

50. ἐπετίμησαν αὐτοῖς is supported by ℵ B C L Δ Ψ 579, 892, 2427 *pc* c k sa^mss and bo. However, A D W Θ *f*¹ *f*¹³ *Majority text* lat sy and Basil of Caesarea support a lengthened reading: ἐπετίμων τοῖς προσφέρουσιν or φέρουσιν. The longer reading probably represents a scribal clarification of who the disciples rebuked.

(ἐναγκαλισάμενος), he placed his hands upon them and began blessing them (κατευλόγει). (Mark 10:13–16)[51]

Questions immediately come to mind. Does this take place in the house? There is no indication they have left it.[52] Who are bringing these children? Are they followers of Jesus? Are they sympathizers or merely people clamoring for a blessing from a holy man, a prophet, or healer? We might presume from the context of "household" that these are parents or caregivers of the children, but Mark does not specify. Nevertheless, these people have agency; the children do not.[53] This leads to a modern interpretive question never asked: Do these children even want to be brought to Jesus?

Why is it important for Jesus to "touch" the children?[54] Gundry has highlighted the importance of touch in Markan healings (3:10; 5:27–34; 6:56; 7:32–35; 8:22–25), exorcisms (7:25–30; 9:17–29), and resurrections (5:41–42). However, these events typically unfold in clear and dramatic ways. If adults were bringing children to Jesus for one of these reasons, Mark would not have missed the opportunity to emphasize it.[55] Derrett argues that Mark's use of the plural "hands" in v.16 signals the touch is about the transference of "charisma by direct touch," whereas touch by one hand signals healing.[56] Meanwhile, whether the children wish to be brought to Jesus or not, Mark quickly reminds readers of their marginal status[57] by way of the disciples' rebuke.

51. Luke (18:15) replaces the initial παιδία with τὰ βρέφη, "babies," ensuring the reader understands them to be infants. The subsequent reference to children in each Synoptic uses τὰ παιδία. None clarify who were bringing the children. On Luke's five uses of τὰ βρέφη, see Légasse, *Jésus et l'Enfant*, 40ff., 195–209.

52. Bailey believes that Mark intends the reader to view 10:13–16 through the lens of 9:35–37, noting that this earlier pericope is set within a household, where one would expect to see a child (Bailey, "Experiencing the Kingdom," 60).

53. Regarding vv. 13–14, Liebenberg notes that children could not demand anything; they were entirely dependent on the kindness of others. The point, however, for Leibenberg is that no one can demand the kingdom. Nor can one receive it unless it is given by someone. For Leibenberg, the blessing that the children receive points to "how it is 'given' and 'what' is given" (Leibenberg, *Language*, 471).

54. Each Synoptic author emphasizes the expectation that Jesus touch them.

55. Gundry, "Children," 150; cf. Bailey, "Experiencing the Kingdom," 61.

56. Derrett, "Why Jesus Blessed the Children," 11.

57. Bailey notes that whereas earlier commentaries focused on the characteristics of children as a key to interpreting this pericope, now they generally focus on their status as marginal members of society (see Bailey, "Experiencing the Kingdom," 58–59, where he

Yet Jesus rebuffs the disciples and accepts children in his presence (Mark 10:14ab; Matt 19:14ab; Luke 18:16ab), a highly unusual action for a teacher of adult learners in the first century.[58] Why? According to Gundry, it is because the kingdom of God of which Jesus spoke *in the Beatitudes* is of special benefit to the "lowly and powerless." Since children share these qualities, he therefore receives them into the kingdom. "Children *qua children* . . . —referring presumably to children within the covenant community—are the intended recipients of the reign of God. It has come for them."[59] To paraphrase Strange, they counted for something in Jesus' ministry. He "was an observer of children" (Matt 11:16–19), and he ascribed "significance" to them in his "message and ministry."[60] For the disciples, Jesus' action should have recalled his inclusive actions and teaching over the "Child in the Midst," but they appear to have quickly forgotten this lesson.

Then, once more, Mark does something seemingly astonishing. He has not only brought children from the social and narrative margins, now he has his messianic protagonist pronounce that children are part of the kingdom of God (v.14c and par.); they are included. Here, the Markan phrase τῶν γὰρ τοιούτων ἐστὶν ἡ βασιλεία τοῦ θεοῦ is more often translated "[F]or the kingdom of God *belongs to* such as these." τῶν τοιούτων is clearly a genitive construction implying possession. However, in an effort to lend greater emphasis to the argument by Gundry and other recent child theologians, I have taken the suggestion of James Francis, and substituted "belongs to" with "consists of."[61] "Belongs to" does not capture the difficulties obscured in what Mark tries to convey. Children were given gifts in antiquity as now, and Mark wants to convince us that the kingdom must be received as a gift, just as children do.[62] It can be argued that the authors' analogy falls short because children in antiquity actually possessed noth-

---

credits Myers as a pivotal figure in this transition).

58. Only Mark gives Jesus' indignant reaction to the disciples. Drawing from social-scientific studies of Mediterranean culture, Perkins reminds readers that young "children should have been with the women, not hanging around the teacher and his students" (Perkins, *Mark*, 637).

59. I italicized "in the Beatitudes" because Gundry combines the Synoptic pericopae in this explanation (Gundry, "Least and the Greatest," 38; Gundry, "To Such as These," 472; Gundry, "Children,"151–52). Read separately, however, the Markan omission of Beatitudes precludes their use as an interpretive lens.

60. Strange, *Children*, 38.

61. Francis, "Children and Childhood," 76.

62. Donahue and Harrington, *Mark*, 300.

ing in themselves, which "belongs to" implies. The patriarchal nature of Greco-Roman and Jewish societies typically functioned as if everyone and everything in a household belonged to the oldest resident male.[63] A gift to a child from his father is one thing, but a gift from a stranger would likely be subject to the approval of the *pater*. Instead, I have chosen, "consists of" because children were a part of social associations, such as families, tribes, phratries, or even mystery cults. Therefore, "consists of" seems more appropriate; it assumes inclusion without the overtones of possession.

Moreover, Best points out that Mark's τῶν τοιούτων carries two possible meanings: "to those similar to children," representing a classical Greek rendering, or "to these children," equivalent to τῶν τούτων, a rendering occasioned in Hellenistic Greek and elsewhere in the New Testament.[64] The latter rendering, of course, advances the "child-friendly" image that Jesus and the Synoptic authors wish to portray. Reading for children in the Synoptics, this rendering emphasizes "how open Jesus was to children"; that he "wanted the children to have as full access to him as adults might have."[65]

At this point, Mark and Luke portray Jesus telling the adults, "Truly I tell you, whoever does not welcome the kingdom of God like a young child (ὡς παιδίον), will never enter it" (Mark 10:15; Luke 18:17).[66] This verse has received significant attention among scholars for two reasons. First, those concerned with redaction, form, or tradition-historical criticism assert the intrusive quality of the verse and point out that Matthew's relocation of the verse demonstrates its secondary nature.[67] As a result of such methods, some are concerned to speculate on the *sitz im leben* of the community/ies behind the text. For example, Müller comments:

---

63. deSilva, *Honor*, 181–85.

64. Best, *Disciples*, 91; see also Légasse, *Jésus et l'Enfant*, 39.

65. Strange, *Children*, 49.

66. Matthew does not include this saying here, but includes a variant in the midst of his pericope on the "Child in the Midst" (Matt 18:3).

67. E.g., Best argues that Mark inserted 10:14c and 15 into a pre-Markan complex consisting of vv. 13–14ab–16 (Best, *Disciples*, 91); and, although its inclusion in Mark stresses the child is a model of kingdom membership, Best writes: "Matthew presumably did not read Mark 10:15 in this way or he would have retained it, since it would then have been no longer parallel to his 18:3; equally, John 3:5 does not reflect this interpretation of Mark 10:15. These facts suggest that in the original meaning of the saying the child was not the model of the Kingdom. Within the Marcan context verse 14c blends more easily with verse 15 on the assumption that the child is the model for reception, which is the generally accepted interpretation." (Best, *Disciples*, 95). Müller provides a very detailed literary analysis of v. 15 (Müller, *In der Mitte*, 52–61).

Wer gehört dazu und wer nicht—zur Gemeinde und damit letztlich zur Basileia, die (schon) angebrochen ist und (in Zukunft) öffentlich erscheinen wird? . . . Der eminent wichtige Konflikt zwischen Juden—und Heidenchristen dreht sich um diese Frage. Die bereits erwähntsn Stellen Lk 11,52 und Mt 23,13 sprechen dieselbe Problematik an. Der Konflikt kann sich auch auf verschiedene Personengruppen beziehen, wie wiederum Mt 11,18f.25ff oder die verschiedentlichen Hinweise auf die "Kleinen" zeigen. Er bezieht sich aber offenbar auch auf Kinder, deren Existenz in der gesellschaftlich-religiösen Beurteilung vornehmlich durch einen Mangel gekennzeichnet war. Es muß vor und in der Zeit des Markus Strömungen gegeben haben, die die Zugehörigkeit zu den Gemeinden reglementieren und damit bestimmte Personengruppen entweder gar nicht oder nicht voll zulassen wollten. . . . Daß dieses Problem eben nicht nur Kinder betraf, zeigt an, daß es sich hier tatsächlich um eine grundlegende Frage urchristlichen Gemeindelebens handelt. Aber es ging *auch* um Kinder, und es ging insofern *besonders* um Kinder, weil bei ihnen die "Mangelexistenz" besonders deutlich hervortrat. Haben sie (und andere, ähnlich "defizitäre" Personengruppen) einen Platz in der Gemeinde und damit auch in der künftigen Basileia?[68]

For Müller then, Mark is confronting an exclusionary policy in his congregation, and the pericope serves a polemical function in favor of inclusivity of children, or any "little one" facing potential exclusion. Second, what aspect of childlikeness is necessary for becoming a kingdom member? Since I am more concerned with the narrative in its final form, most of my focus addresses this question.

Imagine the surprise on the faces of these children, not to mention the adults, when Jesus says kingdom entrance requires that one become ὡς παιδίον. What does this mean? Writing several years ago, Simon Légasse stated: "Parabole humaine, l'enfant, comme type de foi, ne peut être vu que comme celui qui a confiance en plus grand que lui, en l'adulte, en ses parents, en ceux qui représentent pour lui puissance, savoir et secours";[69] complete trust, hope, or dependence are requisite. Following the lead of Willi Egger, Gundry takes this phrase to mean one who is not yet obliged

---

68. Müller, *In der Mitte*, 77.

69. "Humanly speaking, the child, as a model of faith, can only be seen as one who trusts in those greater than him, in the adult, his parents, who represent him for power, knowledge and assistance" (Légasse, *Jésus et l'Enfant*, 193; my translation). Perkins echoes this (Perkins, *Mark*, 647).

to keep the Jewish law, therefore entirely dependent and trusting on God's favor, both of which are "child-like."[70] For some, it refers to one's ability to receive a gift without demanding it.[71]

Most commentators tend to read the Lukan (and sometimes Markan) account through Matthew, where Matthew's "like a young child" clearly means *humility* (Matt 18:2–3). However, as is pointed out in an insightful article by Stephen Fowl, they are very different. First, Fowl argues that entering the kingdom, best interpreted *for Luke* (18:15–17) by the subsequent stories of the rich young ruler (18:18–30), the healing of the blind man near Jericho (18:35–43), and that of Zacchaeus (19:1–10), equals gaining eternal life (18:18, 30), which is also equivalent to being saved (18:26); they refer to the same process. Second, he argues that the process of becoming "like a young child" means a "sudden, single-minded attraction" to Jesus, and the abandonment of any hindrances that would prevent such action.[72] Fowl's reading dovetails with our definition of discipleship set forth in chapter one, since Fowl's interpretation of the latter is contingent upon the agency to follow Jesus.

Yet, as one who intentionally reads the text with "real" children in mind, Ched Myers satirically challenges those commentators who interpret the verse simply in metaphorical terms.

> Is not Jesus' call to "become a child" just a hyperbolic example of status reversal? Surely we are not meant to take him seriously; after all, the whole point of life is to "grow up." Mark must be speaking

---

70. Gundry, "Children," 170–71; "Least and Greatest," 39–40; "To Such as These," 473–74. For Matthew (18:1–5), humility is identified with child-likeness, exhibited "*toward children* on the part of *church leaders* in particular and *for the sake of children* who are at the mercy of those greater than themselves in the community" ("Least and Greatest," 41–42; "To Such as These," 474–75).

71. Liebenberg interprets "being given and receiving" as metaphorical for "*understanding* and *perceiving*" (Leibenberg, *Language*, 472–73); cf. Mann, where he says, "simply, and without any sense of having earned the gift" (Mann, *Mark*, 397); Francis views receiving the kingdom in both Mark and Luke as related to "a sense of glad and wholehearted acceptance" like a child receives a gift (Francis, "Children and Childhood," 76–77).

72. Fowl, "Receiving the Kingdom," 155–58. Strange arrives at much the same conclusion (Strange, *Children*, 52). By contrast, Fitzmyer writes in his Lukan commentary that Luke meant qualities such as "openness, lowliness in society, minority, helplessness, without claim of achievement, and in need of constant maternal and paternal attention." However, true to the warning above about conflating the accounts, Fitzmyer earlier states that the use of children is to teach Jesus' followers about *humility* (*Luke*, 1194; cf. statement at ibid., 1191).

metaphorically here. According to such logic, most commentators do *not* take this text seriously. It is the occasion for passing tributes to the happy innocence of childhood, or appeals to the "child within," or homilies on "Jesus' love for the little children" . . . But what if Jesus means what he says?

He goes on to explain that if Mark uses examples of poor, Gentile, and impure characters to illustrate Jesus' concern for the socially marginalized, why would we not expect him to then use examples of actual children?[73]

Finally, irrespective of the children, they are brought to Jesus by their charges. In Mark, he lifts them up, or embraces them in his arms, and confers a blessing on them. This is where Derrett's article becomes especially important for Gundry. For Derrett, Jesus' blessing in Mark is a symbolic adoption of these children into the kingdom, analogous to the blessing (and adoption) of Joseph through Ephraim and Manasseh by Jacob, their grandfather, in Genesis 48, which reads:

> "Therefore your two sons, who were born to you in the land of Egypt before I came to you in Egypt, *are now mine*; *Ephraim and Manasseh shall be mine*, just as Reuben and Simeon are . . . Bring them to me, please, that I may bless them." . . . So Joseph brought them near to him and he kissed them and embraced (περιελαβεν) them . . . Israel stretched out his right hand and laid it on the head of Ephraim, who was the younger, and his left hand on the head of Manasseh . . . He blessed Joseph, and said, ". . . bless the boys; and in them let my name be perpetuated, and the name of my ancestors Abraham and Isaac." (Gen 48:5–16, NRSV; emphasis mine)

Their blessings bear directly on the messianic expectation, since they represented "the total of the blessings conferred on Abraham, Isaac, and Jacob. The boys will multiply like fish into a multitude in the middle of the earth (48:16). *This at once alerts us to the call of Jesus' fishermen, and there is surely a link.*"[74] Despite Jesus' provenance from Nazareth in Mark, Derrett seeks to link the Jesus-Bethlehem tradition to the prophetic blessings on the sons of Joseph. Adopted now by Jacob, their grandfather, they become his sons. This legal/prophetic action also made them adopted sons of their grandmother, Rachel, whose tomb happens to be in Bethlehem in Judea. In this way, the prophetical blessings of Ephraim and Manasseh may be

73. Myers, *Binding the Strongman*, 267–68.
74. Derrett, "Why Jesus Blessed the Children," 6; emphasis is mine.

linked with Jesus, who (presumably) hails from Bethlehem.[75] This link is important in order to establish: 1) that Jesus' embrace of children brought to him was really a metaphor for, or symbol of, adoption, and 2) therefore, Jesus was concerned about the welfare of children.

Building on Derrett's argument, Gundry points out that the Markan word translated "embrace" (ἐναγχαλίζομαι; in Mark 9:36 and 10:16) suggests the assumption of a "parental role." In support of this reading, she cites the story of Cybele, who took exposed infants up into her arms (ἐναγχαλίζομενον) as a mother goddess, thereby saving them from death (Diodorus Siculus 3.581–583). Also, Plutarch briefly mentions the Roman festival of Leucothea (the Matralia), in which Roman women ἐναγχαλίζονται and τιμῶσιν the children of their sisters (*Moralia* 492D). For Gundry, these examples show that "the women's hug thus symbolizes their readiness to assume a parental role for a niece or nephew in order to save a motherless child from perishing, as did Leucothea." Then, after quoting its use in Mark 9:36–37, she writes:

> Not only love and acceptance . . . of little children but attending to their needs in a more comprehensive sense is suggested by the parallelism of the verbs "hug" and "receive." . . . Jesus' hug, therefore, can be seen as an adoptive embrace, an assumption of a parental role. His subsequent blessing indicates that he has adopted the children in order to pass on an inheritance to them before he dies, and in this way "save" them.[76]

Interpreted in this manner, she links Jesus' actions toward children with the eschatological unfolding of events. His concern is their ultimate destiny.

---

75. Derrett, "Why Jesus Blessed the Children," 7–9. In addition to Gundry, Francis also believes Jesus' blessing of the children might echo the blessing of Ephraim and Manasseh (Francis, "Children and Childhood," 74). Acknowledging there is no direct evidence, Marcus believes Derrett's argument is very plausible and "makes a lot of sense of our passage in its context." For Marcus, Jesus becomes a sort of "godfather" to the children. In support, he notes that Jesus subsequently calls his disciples "children" (10:24) and the term "father" is interestingly absent of humans among Jesus' new fictive family of believers (10:29–30; Marcus, *Mark 8–16*, 717).

76. The reference to Diodorus Siculus, Plutarch, and the block quote are from Gundry, "Children," 156. On page 157, she also references the use of ἐναγχαλίσαμεν in the *Testament of Abraham* 14.28, Manuscript D, where eschatological salvation is linked with a divine embrace. For Donahue and Harrington, Jesus' "hug" shows his "loving acceptance" of children *as model* receptors. His blessing them involved transferring his power to them (Donahue and Harrington, *Mark*, 300; my emphasis).

Their eschatological inheritance aside, she finds Jesus' "hug" in Mark an extraordinary display of "love and affection" in the first century. She juxtaposes the gesture with the overtones of a suffering, exposed infant, through her citation of the letter of Hilarion from Alexandria referenced in chapter two (P. Oxy. 4.744).[77] In fact, Gundry explicitly links the temporal suffering (i.e., weakness/neediness) of the Son of Man with the suffering of exposed infants in the Greco-Roman world. For instance, she argues that by juxtaposing the passion prediction in Mark 9:30–33 with the "Child in the Midst" in Mark 9:35–37,

> We can conclude that Mark intentionally parallels Jesus' identifica-tion with the little child with his self-reference as the suffering Son of Man and that they are mutually interpretive. But what justifies such a parallel? Infants and children were sometimes the objects of . . . the Greco-Roman practice of exposure, or abandonment to death or fate . . . A loose parallel can be drawn to the Son of Man's betrayal into human hands by one of his own . . . It is not too much to assume that Mark's audience would have caught an allusion to the suffering child in Jesus' teaching.[78]

Therefore, according to the Synoptic authors, and particularly Mark, Jesus identifies with children. He taught that the kingdom belongs to them. They are models of entering the kingdom, and models of what it means to be great in the kingdom. Adult followers are told to serve them, and serv-ing children signifies receiving Jesus, and God himself.[79] And although Donahue and Harrington believe the entire pericope tells us more about the kingdom than children, they state in their Markan commentary:

> On the one hand [the passage] shows Jesus' positive concern for children. *He takes children seriously as human persons,* calls atten-tion to the wisdom they display in regarding everything as a gift, and seals his genuine affection for them with an embrace and a blessing.[80]

Meanwhile, although Matthew and Luke lack Mark's "embrace," and therefore, any hint of a symbolic adoption, their respective portrayals of

---

77. Gundry, "Children," 157–58.

78. Gundry, "Least and Greatest," 45; "To Such as These," 477.

79. Gundry, "Least and Greatest," 36; "To Such as These," 470–71.

80. Donahue and Harrington, *Mark*, 301; my emphasis.

the pericope have reinforced the notion that children have unique status in relation to Jesus and the kingdom of God.

> Then young children (παιδία) were being brought to him that he might touch them with his hands; but the disciples denounced them. Then Jesus said, "Let the young children (τὰ παιδία) [come] and do not prevent them from coming to me. For the kingdom of heaven consists of such as these." And he touched them with his hands. He departed from there. (Matt 19:13–15)

> They were also bringing babies (τὰ βρέφη) to him that he might touch them; but seeing it, the disciples denounced them. Then Jesus called to them saying, "Let the young children (τὰ παιδία) come to me and do not hold them back, for the kingdom of God consists of such. Truly I tell you, whoever does not welcome the kingdom of God as a young child (ὡς παιδίον) will never enter it." (Luke 18:15–17)

Real children are placed in relation to Jesus, displacing for a moment the adult disciples. In the words of Keith White:

> Whatever else they may stand for metaphorically, they are real children, and their actual participation in the narrative cannot be allowed to be eclipsed by other readings . . . They are despised and violated if in any way people take flight on the metaphor and abandon the real child.[81]

From White's perspective, the Matthean Jesus was intentionally "committed to the well-being" of children and expressed a genuine interest in them. He would not use a child, or anyone, simply as a symbol for teaching adults. This may happen, of course, but "his primary motivation is love and compassion for the individual concerned."[82] Warren Carter affirms the often metaphorical aspect of "disciples as children," but, like White, also asserts that, taken literally, "it affirms the importance of children in the alternative households of the kingdom," which the lack of a "like a young child" saying in Matthew 19:13–15 permits. As such, it demonstrates Jesus' compassion and mercy toward children.[83] And although Karl-Heinrich

81. White, "He Placed a Little Child," 365.

82. Ibid., 368.

83. Carter, *Households and Discipleship*, 90, 93. In a recent article, Ostmeyer examines the form-critical nature of the Matthean pericope, arguing 19:13–15 is a chiasm that encapsulates Matthean theology using the child-Father relationship, prayer, and

Ostmeyer is primarily concerned with *Formgeschichte*, he concurs that this Matthean pericope focuses on children rather than "disciples as children," stating that Matthew "[R]ückt zugleich das Votum über die Kinder, die Anteil am Himmelreich haben (Mt 19:14), ins Zentrum der Perikope." By contrast, "Bei Markus und Lukas wirkt der Vers wie der Vorspruch zum eigentlichen Höhepunkt, der Aufforderung zur Annahme der Basileia wie ein Kind."[84]

As for the Lukan passage, John Carroll argues that the main point is "the inversion of status and power in the world ruled by God."[85] The adult followers are deliberately set in stark narrative opposition to the children, at the expense of the former. And the juxtaposition of this pericope with the following passage about the rich young ruler further emphasizes the point: infants, who model the kingdom, contrast sharply with the ruler "who cannot enter God's realm, despite his fidelity to Torah—and his status, power, and wealth."[86]

What then have we learned about the characterization of children in relation to Jesus and his eschatological band of followers by the Synoptic authors? The Synoptic authors appear to suggest that children are members of the kingdom of God, and therefore within Jesus' new fictive family in three ways. First, children are spatially and proximally situated near and with Jesus in healing narratives, in his "midst," by touch, and possibly through symbolic adoption. Second, they appear to be included by their positive inclusion in several sayings and teachings about the kingdom. Third, Jesus is portrayed, particularly within the healing, exorcism, and resurrection narratives, as concerned for families, including children, and their restoration. Moreover, several scholars accept this presentation of a "child-friendly" Jesus without much qualification, teasing out creative interpretive threads from a stock of positive images.

---

the kingdom. He notes three main variants related to these verses: (1) Matthew changes Mark and Luke's "that he might touch them" to "lay hands on them and pray" (v. 13); (2) there is no warning in Matthew that one cannot enter the kingdom unless one receives it "as a child"; and (3) Matthew simply says Jesus "went away" after he lays hands on the children (v. 15) (Ostmeyer, "Jesu Annahme der Kinder," 2).

84. Matthew "*places the invitation to the children, who belong to the kingdom of heaven (19:14), at the center of the pericope. In Mark and Luke, the invitation is the prelude to the real climax, the call to accept the kingdom 'as a child'*" (Ostmeyer, "Jesu Annahme der Kinder," 4; my translation).

85. Carroll, "What Then Will This Child Become?," 190n21.

86. Ibid., 190.

The Kingdom, Discipleship, and Families

Clearly from chapter two, children were situated within families or under the supervision of adults, on which they were dependent for food, clothing, and shelter. Since many understand the preceding narratives to portray Jesus seeking out children and their families in order to make disciples of them, to bring them into the kingdom, what type of families does our protagonist encounter in the Synoptic Gospels?

Synoptic Passages on Family

On the one hand, there are references among the Synoptic authors' that acknowledge the foundational institution of the biological family. For example, Matthew and Luke provide genealogical backgrounds for Jesus (Matt 1:1–17; Luke 3:23–38). They attribute to him an ancient Jewish ancestry, which also acts as the messianic "calling card," so to speak, centuries of accumulated honor now ascribed on the human level to Jesus. Furthermore, the nativity accounts serve, at one level, to underscore the fundamental institution of family, with the images of a father, mother, and an infant who is helpless and entirely dependent upon them, and the divine guidance they receive on his behalf (Matt 1:18–25; Luke 2:1–24). The infancy narrative of John the Baptist in Luke can also be read in such manner (Luke 1:5–25, 57–66).

According to our authors, Jesus is confronted as an adult over his teachings by his fellow townspeople of Nazareth. They reference his biological family in a rhetorically derogatory manner. "'Is this not the carpenter, the son of Mary and brother of James and Joses and Judas and Simon; and are his sisters not here with us?' And they were scandalized at him" (Mark 6:3 and par.). In this way, the Synoptic authors clearly know the cultural currency at play with their first-century audience—i.e., the status and occupation of one's family should be a determining factor over one's status in life.

Moreover, the Synoptic authors appear to reaffirm the commandment to "honor your father and mother" as the will of Jesus in at least two places. In Mark 7:9–13 (cf. Matt 15:1–9) some Pharisees and scribes confront Jesus because his disciples have eaten with unwashed hands. Why do the disciples break with the purity traditions, they ask? Then, Jesus charges these Pharisees and scribes with breaking the commandment to honor one's parents in favor of observing added traditions, in this case, vowing certain materials to God that could have been used to support one's parents. Meanwhile, in Mark 10:19 (cf. Matt 19:16–26; Luke 18:18–27) Jesus responds to the rich man seeking eternal life, "You know the commandments: . . . Honor your father and mother," and the Jewish man affirms he has kept them from his youth.

In a recent work, Peter Balla extensively examines these passages in light of the child-parent relationship, arguing that "the early Christians observed both the Fifth Commandment and the commandment to love one's neighbor."[87] At one point, he states that both Matthew and Mark agree that honoring one's parents was "valid and should be observed without looking for reasons for exceptions."[88] Balla notes that the story of the rich man is immediately followed by the disciples' claim that they have left everything including family for the sake of the kingdom. Yet, he believes they have not neglected their duties to what he titles the "Fifth Commandment" while leaving all behind.[89]

Another group of examples are the healing and exorcism narratives where caregivers bring children to Jesus. In both the story of Jairus' daughter (Mark 5:21–24, 35–43; Matt 9:18–19, 23–26; Luke 8:40–42, 49–56) and the daughter of the Syrophoenician woman (Mark 7:24–30; Matt 15:21–28) Jesus restores the life of a young girl to her caregivers. In both narratives, the caregiver desperately seeks help for the child, and in the first story, both father and mother accompany Jesus and some disciples into the room where she lay. Similarly, in the stories of the boy with a demon (Mark 9:14–27; Matt 17:14–18; Luke 9:37–43) and the slave of the centurion (Matt 8:5–13; Luke 7:1–10),[90] the point of the authors is often taken to be about restoring proper household relationships. Furthermore, Matthew and Luke assume that parents naturally desire only good for their children (Matt 7:7–11; Luke 11: 11–13), and Matthew's mention of women and children among those fed miraculously by Jesus could be read as signifying the presence of families among the crowd (Matt 14:21; 15:38). For some, these narratives demonstrate the value and importance of restored family relationships.[91] Moreover, certain parables present dynamic father-son relationships: e.g.,

87. Balla, *Child-Parent Relationship*, 120.
88. Ibid., 119.
89. Ibid., 121.
90. Cf. John 4:46b-54 where the character healed is the centurion's son.
91. Also note the family scene in Jesus' prayer in Luke 11:7.

the parable of the "Wicked Tenants" (Mark 12:1–12; Matt 21:33–46; Luke 20:9–19), Matthew's parable of the two sons (Matt 21:28–30), and the parable of the "Prodigal Son" (Luke 15:11–32).[92]

Finally, Mark and Matthew seem to echo Hellenistic "household codes" in some instances. First, Jesus squares off against some Pharisees and scribes over divorce and remarriage, seemingly emphasizing the "original intent," if I may use such loaded legalese, of Jewish marriage traditions (Mark 10:1–12; Matt 19:1–9)—the husband-wife element of the household codes. Second, the Synoptic authors (now including Luke) turn to the parent-child element of the household code after affirming marriage. Jesus affirms children, blessing those brought to him, presumably by their parents (Mark 10:13–16; Matt 19:13–15; Luke 18:15–17). Third, it is argued that the relationship between, presumably, a head of household and his wealth is the household dimension addressed by the account of the "rich ruler" (Mark 10:17–31; Matt 19:16–26; Luke 18:18–27). Husband-wife, parent-child, and owner-possessions or master-slave, in their own way the Synoptic authors expound on contemporary Hellenistic and Jewish rules of household management.[93]

What should we conclude from this brief survey? In the words of one modern family ministry leader,

> For one thing, we ought to treasure the sweet view of the family with which Christ gifted his church. This sweet view of the family is a higher view of marriage and family than the world offers. It demands the engagement of the men. For another, all of us must recognize the centrality of children in the equation of the family . . . impacted by the gospel, a Christian view of the family magnifies the importance of women and children in the home . . . In Christ, men are no longer to be disengaged from family life—and women and children are elevated from an inferior position.[94]

---

92. In addition to citing each of these examples, Balla also adds the nomenclature of Jewish sons based on their fathers: for example, Bar-Timaeus (Mark 10:46); Simon, father of Alexander and Rufus (Mark 15:21); "the sons of Zebedee" (Mark 10:35/Matt 20:20; Matt 26:37; Luke 5:10; and John 21:2), and he adds, "One wonders whether this would have been possible had they left their father in such a scandalous way that they were regarded as ungrateful children" (Balla, *Child-Parent Relationship*, 121–29). The quote is taken from p. 123.

93. Carter, *Households and Discipleship*. Compare Barton's remark on Jesus and the "fifth commandment" (Barton, *Discipleship and Family Ties*, 82).

94. Baer, "Near the Cross," 3.

Yet, after reviewing several Evangelical popular and academic re-sources, I found a notable paucity of references to family issues from the Gospels. Most cite the Hebrew Scriptures, particularly Genesis, the Pauline corpus, deuteropauline letters, and the General Epistles. For the most part, however, the Gospels (one might substitute "Jesus") are not a major source for family-building resources.[95] Others are more inclusive of teachings from the Gospels, but sound a cautionary tone.[96] A few critical scholars significant to this project offer positive statements on behalf of temporal families from the Synoptic accounts. Stephen Barton concludes that in sup-port of traditional family structures in Mark, the pericope on divorce and remarriage "presupposes the continuing validity—*indeed the radical re-newal*—of household relations, at least in the present age."[97] In other words, for some scholars, families and family relationships, biological and legal, are critical elements of the gospel narratives. They round out the character of the protagonist, serve as minor characters that move the plot along, and function as legal and social points of debate between Jesus, his followers, and his antagonists.

Jesus and His Eschatological Band of Followers and Sympathizers

On the other hand, if one considers the utter dependence of young children on adults, something seems terribly amiss when we read between the lines for real children in their temporal narrative world, and not some eschato-logical flight of fancy.[98] There are numerous places in the Synoptic Gospels

95. Of the nine most recent issues of *Thriving Family* magazine (issues Nov/Dec 2009 to Mar/Apr 2011; *TF* is the successor to *Focus on the Family Magazine*), only one feature article devoted attention to the historical Jesus' teachings or actions related to the family or children. The feature, which centers on the story of Jairus' daughter, is an excerpt from Max Lucado's *Fearless: Imagine Your Life Without Fear* (Lucado, "Fearless Parent-ing," para. 4–6, 15–20). Amidst his discussions on money and divorce, Stephen Grunlan does reference Jesus' teachings, but his book treats the Bible holistically, drawing from several parts to support thematic principles (Grunlan, *Marriage*). Although Balswick and Balswick reference Jesus much more so than Grunlan, they primarily focus on Jesus' empowerment of followers to love unconditionally and live abundantly, and they also draw from the entirety of Protestant scripture (Balswick and Balswick, *Family*).

96. Kovacs, "Faith and Family," 1–39, esp. 24–28; Martin, *Christian Family Values*, 41–48.

97. Barton, *Discipleship and Family Ties*, 122.

98. To remind readers, use of the term "real" is meant to describe relationships by blood, marriage, legal adoption or purchase between a father, mother, children (brothers

in which real, temporal families do not fare well in the narratives; we recall, too, scenes that make the plight of children seem quite precarious, and which are a direct result of the efforts of Jesus and his eschatological movement. How then do the Synoptic authors portray the Jesus movement with families and children foregrounded? Can a general picture be extrapolated?

It is at this point where my analysis draws upon a particular sociological reconstruction to aid my narrative interpretation. I have chosen to rest my literary reading upon Gerd Theissen's sociological model of the Jesus movement because it is the model currently used, critiqued, and built upon by scholars writing on family ties and household in relation to Jesus and the New Testament, especially Stephen C. Barton[99] and Peter Balla.[100] Gundry relies in large part on Richard Horsley's thesis that Jesus' eschatological gathering was a covenant renewal movement among the communities of Galilee, a model that was in part a critique of Theissen's work, as well as Barton's critique of Theissen.[101] I am in dialogue with them as much as anyone. Furthermore, even some who give significant attention to the Gospel of John in reconstructing Jesus' ministry accept the notion of itinerancy and its impractical demands as a chief characteristic of the movement.[102] This being said, I am not making a claim for or against the historicity of this model, it is simply a tool, one which still informs the dialogue on New

---

and/or sisters), and a master and his slaves. Such usage can apply to characters in literary contexts alone, to historical or anthropological contexts. "Fictive" family or kinship will be used to describe associations characterized as family, but without evidence or suggestion of consanguineous or legal relationship, such as a spiritual family (e.g., Mark 3:31–35), whether in literary contexts alone, or historical contexts.

99. Barton, *Discipleship and Family Ties*.

100. Balla, *Child-Parent Relationship*.

101. For Horsley, these Galileans were taking collective efforts to resist disintegrating social and economic forces of encroaching Hellenism. The itinerant aspects of the movement were minimal and temporary; the movement at large aimed instead at strengthening and reinvigorating families and local communities and the relationship built thereupon (Horsley, *Sociology*; Horsley, *Jesus*; Horsley, *Galilee*; Horsley and Hanson, *Bandits*). For both Theissen and Horsley, the term "Jesus movement" is a sociological characterization. Also, Gundry, "Children," 160–61.

102. E.g., see Fredriksen, *Jesus of Nazareth*, 93, where she refers to Jesus' own ministry and his commission of followers to spread the Gospel as a "combination of impractical missionary etiquette and principled itinerancy." As for scholars working particularly with children, Miller-McLemore brings Theissen's radical itinerant model into the discussion in her summary of Sim, "What about the wives and children," esp. 375–82 (Miller-McLemore, "Jesus Loves the Little Children?," 19–21).

Testament families and kinship, on which I shall overlay my deconstructive interpretation.[103]

Theissen's reconstruction posits that within earliest Christianity, there were complimentary social structures: wandering charismatics, their sympathizers, and the bearer of revelation (i.e., the Son of Man).[104] Only the first two structures are necessary for our purposes. One cornerstone of Theissen's sociological reading of the Synoptic Gospels is that:

> Jesus did not primarily found local communities, but called into being a movement of wander charismatics. The decisive figures in early Christianity were travelling apostles, prophets and disciples who moved from place to place and could rely on small groups of sympathizers in these places.

For Theissen, this was no marginal group but instead the movement's core and he emphasizes the radical, even counter-cultural, demands placed on traditional family relationships by the Jesus movement.[105] According to this reconstruction, family ties were often relativized because the demands of discipleship and proclaiming the dawning kingdom of God took precedence, even over one's biological family.[106] In the Synoptic narratives, the core of this "movement" consists initially of Jesus and his constant companions, joined by others after his death, which became marked by its charisma and itinerancy throughout Galilee and surrounding regions. "Rootlessness" is one term that has been used to describe their wandering lifestyle.[107] It

103. For a well-written challenge to the entire Theissen initiated paradigm, but especially the "covenant renewal" arguments of scholars derived from it, see Draper, "Jesus and the Renewal," 29–42.

104. Theissen, *Sociology*, 7.

105. Ibid., 8. For critics, it should be noted that Theissen arrived at his conclusions based on his analysis of the sayings tradition. See also Theissen, "Wanderradikalismus," 245–71.

106. To be clear, this study aims to use terms and themes of kinship and family in literary, historical, and anthropological contexts. Therefore, "family ties" or "familial relations" will be used when necessary to describe "real" (i.e., by blood, marriage, legal adoption or purchase) kinship associations between a father, mother, children (brothers and/or sisters), and a master and his slaves. "Fictive" family or kinship will be used to describe associations characterized as family, but without evidence or suggestion of consanguineous or legal relationship, such as a spiritual family (e.g., Mark 3:31–35).

107. Theissen, *Sociology*, 8–16, 33. The "wandering" aspect is, of course, not unique to Jesus and his followers, Cynics being perhaps the most obvious other example. Yet, certain examples exist even in the Hebrew Bible, e.g., Elijah. One group of prominent scholars have further developed Theissen's theory of cynic-like qualities of the Jesus

is also noteworthy that in the wake of Jesus' eschatological summoning, a significant ascetic movement emerged within early Christianity—not the most persuasive evidence for a uniform Christian valuation of children.

On the other side of this reciprocal relationship were those persons or groups that Theissen calls "sympathizers" in settled "local communities." Because they were still invested in their local communities, they were limited much more by the honor and shame culture that shaped behavior than were the wandering charismatics. Unlike the latter, they remained tied to their families and traditional way of life. Yet, they were crucial to the itinerants because they provided the food, shelter, and ready audience that permitted the latter to continue their alternative lifestyle. The itinerants, in turn, healed their sick and taught them the principles of an otherworldly kingdom. Meanwhile, a crucial point for Theissen is that *sympathizers largely remained within Judaism.*[108] They might have gone out to hear Jesus or an itinerant proclaim the coming kingdom of God, had faith that God could use a holy man to heal their child, or given food and shelter, even regularly, to Jesus or a disciple, but they need not have left Judaism, better, become a "follower" of Jesus in Mark's parlance ("believer" in John's gospel), to do so.

As mentioned in my discussion of the term *discipleship* in chapter one, each gospel has its own criteria for defining what it means to follow Jesus, but a common denominator is that discipleship for the Synoptic authors demands the *agency* to follow and proclaim in the face of persecution and potential death, that one could answer this call. This certainly characterizes Theissen's "wandering charismatics"; less so his "sympathizers." Matthew's conception of discipleship poses the greatest challenge to Theissen's reconstruction, with its simultaneous inclusion of material that reflects an

---

movement, including Vaage, "Q," and Crossan, *Historical Jesus*. However, Luther H. Martin asserts that "wandering" became a characteristic in some ways peculiar to the Hellenistic period. He writes: "The transformation of existence from the social conventions of the polis to a newly articulated individualism, far from being the symbol of possibility and freedom it became for Renaissance Europe, was understood in the Hellenistic world as a problematic, Lucian-like wandering in a greatly expanded world moved by larger forces over which one had no control and of which one had little understanding . . . Hellenistic existence had been propelled into an individualism without instruction, an aimlessness motivated by a profound sense of alienation . . . a crisis of freedom" (L. Martin, *Hellenistic Religions*, 23–24). However, at least one obvious difference for the Synoptic authors is that their heroes are cast with a deliberate sense of purpose and time.

108. Theissen, *Sociology*, 17–23.

itinerant mission, and its emphasis on a community with norms of ethical living in relation to others. Mark best reflects Theissen's model.

Assuming this general picture of a core movement of Jesus and followers, Barton published an excellent study in 1994, *Discipleship and Family Ties in Matthew and Mark*. Carefully exegeting key passages that deal with family relations in the sayings tradition, and deftly using form-critical, redaction, rhetorical, and sociological methods, Barton argues that Jesus was not anti-family *per se* (he relies on this qualifying expression a lot). Instead, the call to discipleship merely subordinated one's family allegiance to the allegiance to one's religious demands. This in itself was actually not unique to the Jesus movement. He cites Josephus, Philo, and texts from Qumran, as well as Stoic and Cynic sources as evidence. What was new is the seeming transference of one's allegiance from God, traditionally defined through one's family and synagogue, to an allegiance of the figure of Jesus and his radical demands of discipleship.[109] For instance, Barton basically argues that the Markan Jesus was not hostile to the idea of family, but temporal familial ties were "strongly relativized" in favor of a new "fictive or spiritual" eschatological family.[110] Likewise, he finds that Matthew supports this overall presentation of the relativization of family ties. In addition to shared Markan material, Matthew's explicitly communal or ecclesiological identity emphasizes that Jesus' followers make up a brotherhood. Additionally, for Matthew Jesus replaces Torah as the object "to be followed and obeyed; allegiance to him transcends every prior allegiance, even one's own blood ties."[111]

For the purposes of the current project, Barton's analyses of pericopae within Matthew and Mark affirm two key points: 1) As portrayed, among the Jesus movement, temporal and biological family relations were negligible in light of the demands of the coming eschatological kingdom; 2) His sociological findings support and complement his literary-critical findings, and vice versa. That is, Barton believes that the Markan and Matthean narratives portray a movement that held a counter-cultural ethos, where discipleship and mission eclipsed any claim to primacy by traditional allegiances to a biologically-centered religious identity. However, where

109. In his words, "it will be seen that discipleship of Jesus poses a threat to family and household ties, since it involves the disciple—every disciple—in a quite fundamental transfer of primary allegiance and commitment" (Barton, *Discipleship and Family Ties*, 20).

110. Ibid., 122–23.

111. Ibid., 218–19.

Barton downplays this tectonic cultural threat by emphasizing the realignment of members within God's new fictive family, I find it appropriate to ask what sort of effects might these narratives posit in the lives of the real (i.e., temporal) characters they portray or assume? How might children in these narratives fair in light of this inimical posturing toward the traditional family structure?

Conclusion

In conclusion, several factors function to convince the reader that children are among Jesus' followers and are included in the kingdom of God. First among these is the spatial /proximal location of children with or near Jesus. The Matthean Jesus' call of the child to him echoes the calling of the disciples (Matt 18:2). The child "in the midst" stands *with* Jesus in contrast to the adult followers as the quintessence of discipleship, even nearer to the status of "learner" than the Twelve, who are depicted as scattering in fear during the passion. The action of Jesus taking children up into his arms is taken by some as a sign of adoption, assuming responsibility for attending to their needs, their protection, and care. Also, Matthew alone situates children among the hearers of Jesus during the feedings of the multitudes. Together, these instances where Jesus focuses his attention on children as children are taken by most child-theologians as examples of Jesus' near unique "love and affection" for them in the period surrounding the first century.

Second, they are included in several sayings and teachings about the kingdom and following Jesus. The Synoptic authors' claims that children are ambassadors of Jesus, and therefore of God, suggest they are members of the kingdom. The teachings to adults about becoming "like a young child," however that is interpreted, is taken by most child-theologians to suggest that the child is "in" in a manner in which the adults need to be, whether that means humble, completely dependent on God, or having abandoned all hindrances. Furthermore, Mark's "for the kingdom of God consists of such like these" is arguably understood as signaling their inclusion.

Third, the portrayal of Jesus' seeming concern for the restoration of children and their families in the healing, exorcism, and resurrection narratives function for some to convey the message that children are included. They are presented as characters in the vanguard of the in-breaking of the kingdom, demonstrating its power to others. For Gundry, they are examples of positive faith responses toward Jesus, by means of their caregivers. In summary, children *as children* are significant members within Jesus' new eschatological gathering. They are among the kingdom's "intended beneficiaries," and are ascribed social parity with adult members.

On the one hand, I agree with Gundry, White, Betsworth, and others that the Synoptic authors challenge the marginalization of children. Challenging their marginal status is certainly *one* way to interpret these texts, and a positive one at that. With respect to children, had the Synoptic authors concluded their accounts of Jesus' eschatological gathering with his blessing of children, then the narrative foregrounding of children as worthy of hospitality and emulation would seem unparalleled. On the other hand, however, the narratives continue; children appear less; Jesus and the disciples move on. The problem as I see it is that their presence has not been fully examined by scholars in light of sayings relativizing family ties, and against the lifestyle indicative of the radical call to discipleship of the broader Synoptic narratives. When one fully considers these factors with children foregrounded over the protagonist, as we will in chapter four, the Synoptic authors' depictions cannot fully obscure the special challenges for children presented by the respective characterizations of Jesus' activity. Furthermore, these aspects of Jesus and his eschatological band of followers might present vexing obstacles for readers who have suffered neglect, abandonment, or the disintegration of their family system as children, particularly where religious identity plays a role.

Given this reading of the narratives, if we take seriously, as modern readers do, the social demands/needs of children, there seems a great disconnect between the Synoptic authors' claims of child inclusion on the one hand, and certain sayings that relativize family ties, the itinerating nature of Jesus' eschatological gathering, and the passion of Jesus in these narratives on the other.

CHAPTER FOUR

CHILDREN AND DISCIPLESHIP IN THE SYNOPTIC GOSPELS

IN CHAPTER THREE WE were reminded that several elements within the Synoptic narratives reveal an undercurrent of domestic turbulence. The call to become a disciple of the protagonist carries a heavy cost, which apparently comes at the expense of family ties. For most of Jewish history prior to the first century, relativizing family ties for the sake of God, was an accepted, if not uncomfortable and troublesome, part of the tradition.[1] However, relativizing family ties to follow a flesh-and-blood figure was not an accepted part of the tradition.

With this as our background, I now offer a different reading of children in the Synoptic Gospels. It is not a pleasant interpretation to ponder, nor a preferred one. Given our focus on the plight of children in the text, if the Synoptic authors go to lengths to portray Jesus so concerned for children that he restores them, embraces them, and desires to be near them, they also depict families within Judaism, broadly defined, deeply affected by discipleship to Jesus. Antagonisms quickly emerge within the stories. Yet, reading for children, who are so dependent on their families or caregivers, how would they fair in such circumstances? In this chapter, I contend that the inclusiveness of children among the disciples and in the kingdom of God by the Synoptic authors is tempered by images of household division and alienation of children as a consequence of Jesus' eschatological gathering of followers. Perhaps unwittingly, the Synoptic authors present a

---

1. In this respect, see the discussion of Abraham, Moses, Phineas and other "Heroic Individuals" sifted from Philo and Josephus in Barton, *Discipleship and Family Ties*, 31–35, 42–44.

disturbing vision with respect to children, where their concern is imbedded in *sayings disruptive of families, the itinerancy of the movement,* and in *the theme of abandonment in Jesus' passion.* When these sayings, plots, and themes are more closely scrutinized, they signal tremendous potential for the detachment of bonds between children and caregivers.

We have yet to question fully the relationship of children to Jesus, the kingdom, and discipleship presented by the Synoptic authors. In order to accomplish this, I undertake a deconstructive reading using the axiom "repeat and undermine,"[2] and take a second look at these texts with an eye toward "teasing out [some] of the conflicting forces of signification at work in the text" outlined by Barbara Johnson, the "ambiguous" and "undecidable" nature of language, "incompatibilities between what a text says and what it does," "incompatibilities between literal and figurative," and "incompatibilities between explicitly foregrounded assertions and illustrative examples or less explicitly asserted supporting material."[3] Within each thematic section, I shall roughly follow the Markan chronology to provide a sense of movement in the shared plot.

Reading for Children—the Problem of Sayings Disruptive of Families

Jesus' True Family

In this section, I read for children within several sayings in light of the eschatological mission of Jesus and his band of followers, particularly against the cost of discipleship. I begin this section with Mark 3:31–35, "Jesus' True Family," and its Synoptic parallels since the saying in v.35 functions like its narrative counterpart[4] to legitimate the theme of familial disruption for the kingdom's sake. Jesus has begun his eschatological movement and already has a crowd of followers around him when he is alerted that his mother and brothers have arrived and are calling for him. However, looking at the followers around him, he tells them, "Here are my mother and my brothers. Whoever does the will of God is my brother and sister and mother" (Mark 3:34b–35; Matt 12:49b–50; Luke 8:21). With this remark the Synoptic

2. Leitch, *Deconstructive Criticism,* 178.

3. B. Johnson, "Teaching Deconstructively," 141–48.

4. That is, the initial calling of the disciples in Mark 1:16–20 and parallels discussed under "itinerancy" below.

authors signal a deliberate separation of temporal families from Jesus' new fictive family, consisting of those who abandon everything to follow him, and the eschatological promises foundational to the movement. The movement consists of those who pledge their allegiance to Jesus and follow him, forsaking even their real families to do so.[5]

As they travel around Galilee for the next several chapters, Jesus and his initial followers seek to increase their new fictive family, attracting male and female disciples (as defined in chapter one) along the way. Increasingly, Jesus reaches out to the socially marginalized, and they become markers of the inclusiveness of the kingdom of God. It is only upon returning to "the house" in Capernaum (Mark 9:33) that Jesus directly raises the question of the possibility of children within the fictive family of discipleship in the kingdom of God in the "Child in the Midst."

The Child in the Midst

> And they came to Capernaum. And being in the house he asked them, "What were you arguing about on the way?" But they remained silent, for on the way they had debated with one another over who was greatest. And he sat down and called the Twelve and said to them, "If anyone wants to be first, he must be last of all and a servant to all." And taking a young child (λαβὼν παιδίον) he placed it in their midst and taking it into his arms (ἐναγκαλισάμενος), he said to them, "Whoever welcomes one of such young children (ἓν τῶν τοιούτων παιδίων) in my name, welcomes me; and whoever welcomes me, does not welcome me but the one who sent me." (Mark 9:33–37)

On the one hand, the child, the vulnerable, lowly, and entirely dependent member of society, is foregrounded by the Synoptic authors. Here, deconstruction's attention to the hierarchical relationships between binary oppositions is instructive. On one level, the Synoptics appear to juxtapose the child with the adult disciples. In a world where adults, and particularly adult males, were valued much more than children, the child is typically the repressed element of the binary opposition, *adult disciples/child*. Yet, the Synoptic Jesus seems to reverse the two, privileging the child over that of the adult male disciples. The disciples are de-centered by the child who

5. Of course, Mark also includes in 3:19b-21 an account of Jesus' family going out to restrain him in the face of allegations that he is disturbed or possessed.

is now "in their midst"; the authors make the child an exemplar of the kingdom, privileged above the momentarily excluded adult disciples. Furthermore, children are ambassadors of the kingdom, identified with Jesus himself. The relationship now appears *child/disciples.*

Meanwhile, interesting issues come into play when we juxtapose the figures of Jesus and the child (παιδίον). "Jesus" is, of course, the Greek form of Joshua, meaning *"The Lord Saves."* παιδίον is a diminutive form of παῖς, meaning "boy," or "child." It can also be translated "slave" or "child slave." However, the verbal derivative of παῖς is παίζω, meaning "to act in a child-like or childish fashion," "to play," "to dance," "to jest," "to mock"; and παιδία can mean "play" or "jest."[6] Thus, "child" in the Greek is linguistically associated with play and the "childish" behavior of the young. In one sense therefore, the concept of salvation is associated with "play" by the "playful" translation of the name "Jesus."

However, there is something vexing about this pericope in particular, where the slippery nature of language makes images ambiguous. Although we child theologians want to assert that this text should be read with children foregrounded, the double meaning lingers. Because παῖς can refer also to a slave, or a child slave, to privilege children would make us likewise guilty of placing slaves *"sous rapture."* The pericope clearly attempts to illustrate servanthood to the adult disciples who are so consumed with status in the dawning kingdom. Read *"slave"* for παῖς, Jesus seemingly centers a "slave" or "child slave," suggesting enslavement is somehow exemplary of the kingdom of God.

Meanwhile, if we return to privileging "child" over "slave," the language of παίζω/παῖς conjures a social world reminiscent of John's gospel, filled with imagery of abundance and merriment, particularly in the festive atmosphere of the wedding at Cana. For in Mark 9:36–37 (and par.), *"The Lord Saves"* puts "play" into their midst; playfulness is privileged over the learning of the learners. Since παίζω can also mean "to mock" or "to jest," it now seems ironic those followers who were just in the midst of a debate over which among them is greatest now stand on the periphery while a mocking figure stares back at them from the arms of Jesus. Again, the relationship appears to be *child/disciples,* the former signifier being the privileged, and the latter repressed—or is it? For while the child remains centered with Jesus in Mark and Matthew, these author almost immediately begin warning those listening not to scandalize "one of these little ones" (Mark 9:42; Matt

6. "παίζω," *TDNT*: S. 5:625–30.

18:6, 10, 14; cf. Luke 17:2). In the midst of these warnings, the child seemingly gets de-centered, marginalized once again in favor of adult disciples.

'One of These Little Ones'

The child is still being held by Jesus in the Capernaum home in Mark when the disciples tell him about an exorcist unaligned with them, whom they tried to stop. But Jesus answers that any help by a stranger, even the hospitality of a cup of cold water offered to the disciples "since you are of Christ's name," is welcomed (9:38–41); do not turn down the support of sympathizers. Then, his attention seemingly turns back to the child in his arm, and he unexpectedly warns them,

> And whoever might scandalize one of these little ones (ἕνα τῶν
> μικρῶν τούτων)[7] that believe in me,[8] it is much better for him if
> a millstone of a donkey was set around his neck and he was thrown
> into the sea. (Mark 9:42)

Do nothing to cause a little one who trusts in him to falter. Does this child believe *in him*? If so, in what capacity does the child believe in Jesus? On this, Mark is silent. The NRSV translates σκανδαλίσῃ as "put a stumbling block before." Even worse, the NIV reads: "cause . . . *to sin*." The wording, particularly, of the latter translation unwittingly turns the little ones into perpetrators of wrongdoing as well. However, in the recent wake of the vast numbers of child sexual abuse cases, both revealed and still hidden, *within the Church*, perpetrated by God's adult ambassadors, perhaps the word "scandalize" should be retained. After this teaching, Jesus went south to Judea and across the Jordan (Mark 10:1).[9]

The use of "one of these little ones" is much more complex in Matthew because this gospel has multiplied the occurrences of the phrase and has moved the first occurrence into a different context than the "Child in the Midst."

---

7. Τούτων is replaced with μου in W, while the following manuscripts simply omit τούτων altogether: K Γ Ψf^{13} 892 and *Majority text*.

8. εἰς ἐμέ receives strong attestation (A B L W Θ Ψ f^1 f^{13} syr^s cop^{sa} *al*). Yet their absence from ℵ D and Δ, and the fact that their inclusion is explicable by means of scribal emendation to Matthew, leaves doubt that they were original to Mark.

9. Concerning Mark's use of σκανδαλίσῃ, Myers suggests the author uses the term in a technical sense to mean causing one to reject the message of the kingdom (6:3) or forsaking the way (14:27, 29; Myers, *Binding the Strongman*, 262).

After the Matthean Jesus raises the synagogue leader's daughter and itinerates throughout Galilee (9:35–37), he commissions the Twelve to proclaim the gospel throughout Galilee, avoiding Samaria, and warns them the message will bring turbulence (10:1–39). However, sympathizers who provide hospitality will be rewarded.

> Whoever welcomes you welcomes me, and whoever welcomes me welcomes the one who sent me. Whoever welcomes a prophet in the prophet's name gets what is due a prophet. And whoever welcomes a righteous person in the name of a righteous person will receive what is due to a righteous person. But whoever might give a single cold cup[10] to drink to one of these little ones (ἕνα τῶν [μικρῶν τούτων])[11] in the name of a disciple, truly I tell you, he will not lose what is due him. (Matt 10:40–42)

In this context, it is immediately clear that "one of these little ones" refers to those commissioned to spread the gospel—i.e., adult disciples.[12]

With this in mind, we segue forward to Capernaum in Matthew 18 again, and the "Child in the Midst." Recall, "Whoever welcomes one such child in my name, welcomes me" (18:5). Then, with the child still present before them, the Matthean Jesus' issues his ominous warning.

> But whoever might scandalize one of these little ones (ἕνα τῶν μικρῶν τούτων) who believe in me, it would be better for him that a heavy donkey millstone was hung around his neck and he might be drowned in the depth of the sea. . . . See not to despise one of these little ones (ἑνὸς τῶν μικρῶν τούτων), for I tell you, their angels in heaven always see the face of my father in heaven . . . Thus, it is not the desire before your Father in heaven that one of these little ones (ἕν τῶν μικρῶν τούτων) is lost. (Matt 18:6, 10, 14)

---

10. D lat sy^{s.c} co; Or and Cyp clarify the cup's contents by adding "water" immediately before ψυχροῦ.

11. D replaces μικρῶν with the superlative form ελαχιστων, from ελάσσων, which similarly can mean *the fewest, least, smallest,* or *worst*. The entire Latin manuscript tradition follows Bezae, with 1424 and a few others simply appending των ελαχιστων to the better attested μικρῶν τούτων. See LS, "ελαχιστος," 214.

12. Müller, *In der Mitte*, 212; Barton, "Jesus-Friend," 35; Boring, *Matthew*, 263; Albright and Mann translate our phrase to read "the most insignificant of these" (*Matthew*, 129); For Légasse, the "little ones" refers to inferior missionaries who should, nevertheless, be received warmly by their Christian peers because they are still Christian disciples (*Jésus et l'Enfant*, 84–85). In each case, they are identified as early Christian missionaries of Matthew's day.

Because of its juxtaposition with the "Child in the Midst," it is entirely within the realm of possibility to view the "little ones" (μικροι), particularly in Mark and Matthew, as referring to children. By reason of this juxtaposition, the authors appear, on the one hand, to encourage such an interpretation. Indeed, Müller agrees that the contextual linking of Matt 18:1–5 with 18:6ff suggests a connection between μικροι and παιδίων.[13] Gundry has pointed out that since τὰ παιδία in Matt 18:1–4 and ἓν τῶν μικρῶν τούτων in 18:14 are both neuter in gender, Matthew associates the two. By contrast, the masculine form ἕνα in 18:6 (cf. Mark 10:42) disrupts the two neuter uses, introducing a potentially broader application. Therefore, she summarizes:

> [W]hether this text refers explicitly or implicitly to children—its relation to the preceding [18:1–5] is clear ... Jesus' warning against mistreating the "little ones" and his instructions to receive little children in childlike humility are two sides of the same coin.[14]

However, most commentators, particularly due to Matthew 10:42, read "little ones" in Matthew 18:6ff; Mark 9:42; Luke 17:2 as Christian "missionaries" or adult followers of Christ.[15] For instance, despite the presence of children in 9:35–37, Mark has Jesus tell the Twelve, "whoever gives *you* a cup of water," where "you" clearly refers to adult believers (9:41).[16]

---

13. Müller, *In der Mitte*, 203.

14. Gundry, "Least and the Greatest," 42; "To Such as These," 475.

15. Regarding their narrative unfolding, Strange asks: "[H]ow far, and in what places, was Jesus speaking literally of children . . .?" He concedes that Matthew's use of "little ones" suggests that "receiving" means "taking an itinerant disciple into one's home," so they are probably not children. Still, he argues that the usurpation of "children" by adults among commentators on these verses has clouded the interpretation of other passages (e.g., the New English Bible and the Revised English Bible's translations of Matt 11:25 and Luke 10:21, where νηπιοι is translated "the simple"; Strange, *Children*, 55–56). Boring asserts that the subject in Matt 18:6 shifts to "members of the Christian community who are immature in faith." In a footnote, he states that the term "children" soon became a designation among early Christians for "ordinary" believers (Heb 2:13–14; 1 John 2:13, 18, 28; 5:21). The entire thrust of Matt 18:6–14, therefore, is that one should not do anything that might hinder the discipleship path of any weaker members of the community (Boring, *Matthew*, 374–75). For Carson, these verses are not about literal children, but refer to those adults "who humble themselves to become like children and are Jesus' true disciples" (Carson, "Matthew," 84).

16. For the Markan text, Marcus argues persuasively that "little ones" should probably be understood as a reference to the Christian community rather than children (Marcus, *Mark*, 689). Also see Müller, *In der Mitte*, 261–69. Donahue and Harrington understand "little ones" in Mark 9:42 to refer to "simple believers" in Christ (*Mark*, 287), while Myers

Meanwhile in Luke, "little ones" appears to mean those attempting to actively follow Jesus,[17] such as the disciples to whom he speaks.

> It is inevitable for scandals to come, but woe to the one by whom they come; it would be better for him if a millstone were hung around his neck and he were thrown into the sea than one of these little ones (τῶν μικρῶν τούτων ἕνα) might be scandalized (17:1–2).[18]

Appearing as disconnected from Luke's "Child in the Midst" as it does, his rendering is even more succinct than that of Mark, and entirely disconnected from any reference to children. He omits any connection to receiving a cold drink. Furthermore, rather than a more concrete teaching about scandal, he narrates only the proverbial, "It is inevitable for scandals to come" (cf. Matthew 18:7). As such, most commentators view this verse in Luke as unrelated to children.[19]

---

discusses them in terms of powerless believers within the Markan community, not as children (*Binding the Strongman*, 263).

17. Culpepper, *Luke*, 321. Fitzmyer finds this saying and the three following it seemingly unrelated to the preceding narrative material and what follows. Similarly, the only element that loosely binds this saying to the follow three is their bearing on discipleship (Fitzmyer, *Luke*, 1136).

18. After Luke's pericope on the "Child in the Midst," there is a lengthy series of teachings, healings, and confrontations throughout Galilee, Samaria, and Judea before we come to his reference to scandalizing "one of these little ones." He is rejected by a Samaritan village (9:51–56), commissions seventy disciples to proclaim the gospel ahead of him (10:1–12), visits the sympathizers Mary and Martha (10:38–42), and in much sharper succession he engages in teachings and confrontations that draw attention to the great reversal of values inaugurated by the apocalypse of the kingdom of God. He denounces Pharisees and lawyers (11:37–54), warns of hypocrisy (12:1–3), of divisions, the cost of discipleship, and draws contrasts between the poor, who are closer to God, and the rich, who are nearer the flames of torment (11:37–16:31). In the unfolding plot, Luke has quickly developed through 16:14–31 what Luke Timothy Johnson describes as "a series of sayings and a parable that together indicted [the Pharisees] of a false legal piety," leading ordinary Jews from the path of true piety (L. Johnson, *Luke*, 260). Given the variety of material leading to this saying, those who might bring scandal may refer to the false legal piety of the Pharisees or other Jewish leaders, or perhaps the rich, who could similarly exhibit a false piety by material means. The fact that Jesus is clearly warning his followers after having just delivered scathing rebukes against outsiders seems to bear out this interpretation.

19. Fitzmyer thinks perhaps the phrase plays off of Luke 10:21, which speaks of "small children," and also evokes a sense of helplessness (*Luke*, 1136–37). Liefeld represents an exception, but clearly reads the Matthean version into Luke: "The 'little ones' would seem to be either young or new believers (cf. Mt 18:1–6) or people whom the world takes little notice of" ("Luke," 267).

Since the Markan and Matthean narratives continue to suggest the child centered "in their midst" is still present during these discussions over "little ones," the authors leave the reader questioning whether the children are metaphors for adult disciples or literal characters in their own right. What is explicitly and implicitly foregrounded? Where some interpreters would rather see the inclusion of children more explicitly foregrounded for theological reasons, the great reversal of social status in the gospels that seems to permit this maneuver may here be turned back over on itself. That is, what we began to see as a *child/disciples* relationship appears to resemble instead a *disciples/child* relationship once again, as the "little ones" who are not really "little ones" (i.e., young children) are instead adult disciples; the child is re-marginalized. If for a moment we were becoming convinced children are kingdom members, the texts themselves begin to bring this into question.

'Let the Little Children Come to Me'

> And they were bringing young children (παιδία) to him so that he might touch them. But the disciples denounced them. But watching, Jesus became irate and said to them, "Let the young children (τὰ παιδία) come to me, do not hold them back, for the kingdom of God consists of such like these. Truly I tell you, whoever does not welcome the kingdom of God like a young child (ὡς παιδίον), will never enter it. And having taken them into his arms (ἐναγκαλισάμενος), he placed his hands upon them and began blessing them (κατευλόγει). (Mark 10:13–16)

Returning for a deconstructive reading of "Let the Young Children Come to Me," where little children are brought to a protagonist entirely accepting of them, we find Jesus touching them or raising them up into his arms, and blessing them (Mark 10:13–14b, 16; Matt 19:13–14b, 15; Luke 18:15–16b). He then tells his immediate followers that the kingdom of heaven consists of such like the children brought to him, and that kingdom entrance requires a state of "child-likeness" (Mark 10:14c-15; Matt 19:14c; 18:3; Luke 16c-17).

However, unlike the healing narratives, here it is the unnamed "other," presumably adult caregivers, that introduce "play" to the protagonist in the pericope. In the rigor of the teacher/disciple relationship, however, there is little room for childish play; the learners refuse to permit the foolishness of παιδία/παῖς/παίζω[20] in the presence of their esteemed teacher.

There may also be some intertextual cues significant for the Synoptic authors in Isaiah 8:16–9:7 where the divine message of Isaiah and the "children" given him[21] has been rejected by Israel. As a result, Isaiah is instructed by the god of Israel to seal up the teachings of God in the face of the idolatry and stubbornness of the people. "Behold, I and the children that the Lord has given me are signs and omens in Israel from the Lord of hosts who lives on Mount Zion" (8:18).[22] This passage may also be echoed in Matthew and Luke where, after condemning the lack of repentance in the Galilean cities of Korazin and Bethsaida, Jesus thanks God for hiding "these things from the wise and intelligent, but have made them known to νηπίοις" ("small children" or "infants"; Matt 11:25; Luke 10:21). Yet despite the instructions given to Isaiah, God promises those in the midst of darkness the sign of a child born who will reign in Zion with righteousness and everlasting peace (9:1–7). Thus, children figure prominently in some of the messianic passages of the Hebrew prophets. Even where they may not directly quote one of these passages, the Synoptic authors have clearly drawn upon the child motif of the prophetic literature as an important sign of the apocalypse of the kingdom of God.

Meanwhile, Jesus welcomes "play" over the objection of the disciples (Mark 10:14 and par.). "Let the *playful ones* come to me"; let *childishness, merriment, jesting,* and *dance* enter among us[23]; "for the kingdom of God consists of such like these" (v.14c). With v.15, Mark (Luke 18:17) emphatically declares that those who refuse to accept the dawning kingdom with a sense of "childishness" or "play" will never enter it (cf. Matt 18:3). In Mark alone, Jesus then embraces "childish things" or "playful ones," physically engaging them with his hands, and praising or blessing them.

For Gundry, the "Child in the Midst" and "Let the Little Children Come to Me," with the healing narratives, collectively portray "Jesus as overcoming the religious and cultural obstacles to embracing children's full and equal participation in the eschatological reign of God."[24] "Taken

---

20. παιδία carries the notion of "childishness" (Oepke, "παίζω," *TDNT* 5:626).

21. Probably disciples of the prophet; see Isa 8:16.

22. Hebrews 2:13 concretely links this verse with early Christian traditions about Jesus.

23. LS, "παίζω," 512; cf. Oepke, "παίζω," *TDNT* 5:626.

24. Gundry, "Children," 143.

together, [these texts] show small or young children as occupying a significant space in Jesus' public ministry."[25] Part of my disagreement with this
characterization lies in what she refers to as "children's full and equal participation" in the kingdom. For her, the emerging kingdom brings "blessing
and deliverance from oppression" for *its subjects*. She capitalizes on the relationship between the kingdom and children characterized in the genitive
construction of "to such as these" (τῶν τοιούτων; Mark 10:14c) to show the
kingdom is theirs, and that is certainly what the authors intend to convey.[26]
They are model recipients, for they do nothing, not even receive it; they
merely submit to its benevolence for the weak and helpless. I would add
they introduce "play" into the kingdom.

In the last chapter I described Derrett's argument that Jesus' embrace
and blessing in Mark can be read as an adoption motif, and that Gundry
derives from this Jesus' assumption of a parental role. Gundry's final point
ties this theme of adoption and parental responsibility solely to the eschatological inheritance that Jesus will pass on to them when he dies, thereby
"saving them." "By a hug and a blessing . . . Jesus claims the little children
brought to him as his own children and mediates an inheritance of salvation to them."[27]

On the one hand, these interpretations seem convincing. The Synoptic
authors center the child, seemingly de-centering the adult disciples. Children appear fully included within the kingdom of God, identified with the
traits of exemplary discipleship. Or, we might say that the authors appear
to privilege παιδία/παῖς/παίζω, i.e., those things associated with being a
child–playfulness, childishness, a "mocking figure," a general lack of *gravitas*—over the serious and seemingly calculating gestures and disputations
of the learners.

This is surprising given that the irrationality of childhood was considered unbecoming of adults, particularly males. Privileging the rationality
of adult reasoning and behavior over that of children, Seneca describes the
rationality of adults over the irrationality of children as a fundamental "difference of quality."[28] Paul tells the Corinthians that when he was a child
(νήπιος), he thought, reasoned, and spoke like one; but when he became a

---

25. These quotes are in direct reference to the portrayal of children in the Gospel of
Mark (ibid., 148), but might be broadly applied to Matthew and Luke as well.

26. Ibid., 151.

27. Ibid., 157.

28. Seneca, *Ep.* 33.7.

man (ἀνήρ), it was time to leave childish ways behind (1 Cor 13:11). Even Matthew and Luke depict Jesus comparing the antics of children to the unresponsiveness of "his generation": This generation is like "children sitting in the marketplace and calling to one another, 'we played the flute for you but you refused to dance. We sang a song of grief, but you refused to mourn'" (Matt 11:16–17; Luke 7:31–32). Commenting on the relationship between the historical Jesus and children in this passage, William Strange believes:

> Jesus was . . . a realist about human nature; he was equally realistic about the nature of children . . . he knew how children, in their play, act out roles in which they exercise power over others . . . There was . . . no sentimentality in Jesus' view of children.[29]

On the other hand, incompatibilities immediately emerge that begin to hint at the problematic nature of child discipleship. First, in Matthew Jesus tells us that the kingdom consists of such children, but after welcoming them so warmly and making such a point of it by laying his hands on them, Jesus disengages from them. In the words of Matthew, he simply "went away" (19:15). Mark is taken by some as indicating Jesus adopts these kids, and yet the same children in Matthew's story are just *left behind by Jesus*.[30] I would suggest that Jesus' hasty departure, literarily, vitiates the adoptive reading of Gundry and Derrett. If one were to embrace their adoption motif, it would require, at the very least, some acknowledgement of, and explanation for, the apparent callousness of Jesus' behavior. Second, despite the apparently sublime indications in the previous narratives that children can become part of this fictive family of disciples, that the kingdom is child inclusive, there is a bewildering gap between the *realia* of Jewish and Hellenistic-Roman society, where children could not leave their families behind to join voluntary associations like Jesus' eschatological band, and the social world conjured by the Synoptic authors. Each of the Synoptics follows this pericope with the story of the "Rich Young Ruler" (Mark 10:17–22; Matt 19:16–22; Luke 18:18–23). What must one do to become a kingdom member, he asks? Jesus tells him, "come and follow me," an action requiring the independence and agency within the narratives which children do not have. In the end, Jesus leaves the "playful ones" behind. There is in fact a *gravitas* to the mission he introduces that leaves play and merriment aside.

29. Strange, *Children*, 50–51.

30. Mark characterizes Jesus here as resuming his journey (10:17).

To underscore this often overlooked estrangement between children and what it means to follow Jesus in the Synoptic Gospels, children are also projected to become the victims of the "Cost of Discipleship" (Mark 13:12–13; Matt 10:21–22; Luke 21:16–17) to households. One day on the Mount of Olives, a few of the disciples ask Jesus privately, in Mark and Matthew, about the signs of the eschaton and what to expect. Luke, however, suggests this is a very public discussion.[31] Among Jesus' reply is the assertion: "Brother will give up brother to death, and a father his children, and children will rise up against parents and have them killed, and you will be hated by everyone because of my name." In other words, you cannot even trust your own family, and in the days of the siege of Jerusalem, "Woe to those who are pregnant and who are nursing infants in those days" (Mark 13:17; Matt 24:19; Luke 21:23). The tectonic shifts brought about by the apocalypse of the kingdom of God and those reacting against it threaten the very existence of infants and fetuses. In Luke's words, nursing and pregnant mothers "will fall by the edge of the sword, and be taken prisoner" (Luke 21:24).

Taking a cue from some child theologians such as Gundry and White, let us step into the narrative for a moment and suppose a few children are among Jesus' "followers" in this pericope. Or, perhaps there are some children within the hearing of Jesus, maybe in the form of Theissen's "sympathizers." What images or thoughts pass through the mind of a child in the narrative when he or she hears a teacher say that one day soon a father will give up his children to have them killed?; that children will have their parents killed? At what period of growth does a child begin to understand hyperbole, sarcasm, metaphor, or any number of linguistic devices used to interpret a teaching? Although the use of τέκνα in these passages most likely indicates adult children, it does not by definition exclude young children.[32] Given our supposition, such a saying would likely seem quite disturbing or troubling to many young minds. Or, perhaps the saying comforts and legitimates the actions of those children now in the kingdom, which left their caregivers back in Perea and became followers, if we could imagine such a thing.

31. Luke tells us in 19:48 and 20:45 that he spoke to his disciples where all the people could hear. In fact, from Luke 19:45 through chapter 21, Jesus is in the temple teaching publicly. Cf. the statement about the privacy of the disciples' inquiry in Matt 24:3 and Mark 13:4, where the latter seems to limit the scope of the discussion further by naming only four disciples, yet nowhere indicates he is only speaking to the Twelve.

32. See Oepke, "τέκνα," *TDNT* 5:637–39.

Perhaps Peter, who is clearly married (Mark 1:30–31), is saddened by the thought of his own children as he reflects on the cost of following Jesus for the relationship of some disciples with their own fathers. In the Synoptic version of Jesus' new fictive family, there are no fathers, except God alone. Still, as a potentially absent husband and father for his "real" family, is he sowing seeds of resentment in his own children? Clearly, the Synoptic authors suggest in Mark 13:12–13 (and par.) that some children will suffer as victims of the cost of discipleship, as family rifts emerge along the fault where one parent has chosen to follow Jesus, and another remains firmly within non-Christian Judaism. For Mark, the breaches are primarily generational.[33]

Near the end of Matthew's "missionary discourse" in Galilee (10:1–11:1), Jesus alludes to Micah 7:6 as he warns the Twelve privately about the vexing costs his disciples will face, even at the most basic social level, the family, as they proclaim the gospel. "For I have come to set a man against his father and a daughter against her mother, and daughter-in-law against her mother-in-law, and a man's enemies will be of his own household" (Matt 10:35–36; Luke 12:52–53). These household divisions foretold by Micah, which the Synoptic authors appropriate, bear real costs where the new fictive family of Jesus' kingdom challenges traditional patriarchal loyalties to the god of Israel, experienced through Judaism and the head of one's household.

> Whoever loves father or mother over me is not worthy of me; and whoever loves son or daughter over me is not worthy of me, and whoever does not take his cross and follow me is not worthy of me. (Matt 10:37–38)

Close attention shows that, like Mark, Matthew casts such confrontation primarily in generational terms. On the other hand, Luke's narrative is even more confrontational, includes splits between spouses, and is directed to an entire crowd of followers:

> And many crowds followed him, and he turned to them and said, "If anyone comes to me and does not hate his father and mother and wife and children and brothers and sisters, even his own life, he cannot be my disciple." (Luke 14:25–26)

Meanwhile, near the end of his discourse on divorce and remarriage, the followers of the Matthean Jesus question his strict judgment; it seems

---

33. For Luke, such breaches include those of husband and wife, as 14:26 indicates.

better to them to remain unmarried (19:10). Then, in a saying unique to Matthew's gospel, Jesus answers: "For there are those who were born eunuchs, and there are eunuchs who have been made eunuchs by men, and there are eunuchs who have made themselves eunuchs because of the kingdom of heaven" (19:12). For Matthew, this reads like a positive development in the unfolding eschatological narrative. Yet, Jesus' blessing of the children follows immediately on the heels of this statement in Matthew. So, while the Synoptic authors have Jesus take time to welcome children, bearing new children is not a priority in the portrayals of Jesus' eschatological movement, nor in writings of the Apostle Paul, both of which quickly give birth to a vast strain of celibacy within early Christianity.[34] Both, in addition, operate under an imminent eschatological expectation, which segues to one more saying in Matthew in which infants and children are projected by Jesus to become victims in the destruction of Jerusalem at the end of days. This saying is linked to Jesus' proclamation of the coming Son of Man. "Woe to those who are pregnant and who are nursing infants in those days" (Matt 24:19; Mark 13:19; Luke 21:23).

In one way or another, these sayings are intricately tied to the eschatological underpinnings of each gospel. Read in this manner, the emerging chasm between older forms of Judaism and this new eschatological sect of Judaism threatens the bonds of traditional temporal families affected by decisions to follow Jesus. When one reads carefully for real children, we become mindful of the shadows left behind by children neglected for the eschatological dream, these places in the text where you can almost hear the Synoptic authors whisper the unfortunate consequences of the gospel: *Make no mistake; children are going to get pinched. They might be forced to take sides with one parent or the other. They might grow to develop their own ideological rift with their parents.* Or, I would add, they might be neglected or abandoned by parents for the sake of the gospel, as evidenced by the story of Perpetua's infant just a few centuries later.[35] Increasingly, there

34. After Paul and the Synoptics Gospels, early Christian emphasis on celibacy begins to emerge in force in writings of the second and third centuries. It is obviously present in early works such as the person of Ignatius of Antioch and in the Gospel of Thomas, and even takes the form of doctrine in many early Christian works such as the *Book of Thomas the Contender*. For critical editions of this text and several others stressing Christian celibacy, see Schneemelcher, *New Testament Apocrypha*. For examples of secondary sources, see Brown, "Bodies and Minds," 129–39; Brown, *Body and Society*; Clark, "Anti-familial Tendencies," 356–79.

35. Martyred in Carthage because of her faith, during the reign of Septimius Severus, Perpetua was permitted to nurse and care for her infant in prison. Yet, she did not

seems a substantial disconnect between the child-inclusive movement of which the Synoptic authors try to convince us, and what a close reading actually permits.

Reading for Children—the Problem of Itinerancy

Discipleship over Family Ties: the Call Narratives

> And passing by the Sea of Galilee, he saw Simon and Andrew, the brother of Simon, casting a net into the sea; for they were fishermen. And Jesus said to them, "Follow me, and I will make you become fishers of men." And immediately they left the nets and they followed him. And a little farther he saw James, son of Zebedee, and John, his brother, and they were in a boat mending the nets. And immediately he called to them and they left their father Zebedee in the boat with the hired servants and followed him. (Mark 1:16–20)[36]

I begin this section on itinerancy with the calling of the first disciples because discipleship had a cost in the Synoptic Gospels that usually does not resonate in today's society. And while the call narratives may remind readers of the cost of discipleship to those who freely choose to become followers, we usually do not consider how discipleship impacts the wives and children they leave behind. What would be the impact if one or both parents accept the call to discipleship in these gospels?

How disgraceful the behavior of James and the other disciples might have seemed to their children, not to mention the deficit in necessary provisions their absences must have caused for their own families. Interestingly, there are almost no references in early Christian texts to suggest that the children of the disciples named in the canonical gospels became followers too.[37] As Barton has shown, one's biological family gives way to the new fictive eschatological family of Jesus.

---

yield to her father's pleas to forgo dying for her faith, even for the sake of her infant. See Ehrman, "Martyrdom," 43–44.

36. Matthew follows Mark quite closely (Matt 4:18–22). Luke provides a much more extended calling (Luke 5:1–11).

37. Eusebius (*Hist. eccl.* 3.30–31) references a letter of one Clement, and a letter of Polycrates, which mentions that the Apostle Philip had daughters who remained models of Christian chastity into old age. The former reference mentions two daughters; the latter mentions three. He then cites a *Dialogue* of Gaius where it is said Philip had four

Why should we entertain speculations about the children of disciples? If as child theologians we purport to take seriously the plight of children today, as well as in the text, then we owe the same concern even to those children who appear just off of the page. In the language of deconstruction, "Because the structure of the sign is determined by the 'trace' or track of that other which is forever absent, the word 'sign' must be placed 'under erasure.'"[38] In other words, part of what makes a disciple (the "sign") in the Synoptics consists of what he or she must leave behind (the "trace"). Therefore, by submitting the disciples to "erasure," the "trace" becomes foregrounded[39]–and given proper attention, there are traces that the Synoptic authors have failed to fully obscure.

The Synoptic authors claim at the outset of Jesus' movement that he has called followers from their temporal familial ties into a new fictive familial structure of which the kingdom of God consists (Mark 1:16–20 and par.). This is affirmed by the juxtaposition of these two conflicting "realities" for the protagonist himself (Mark 3:31–35 and par.). However, our particular "traces" flicker within the narrative in only a few places. In Matthew 10:37 and Luke 14:26, Jesus confronts his followers with one of the ultimate costs of discipleship, forsaking even one's τέκνα.[40] At this point, the authors seem to imply that followers of the protagonist have indeed left children behind. Then our "traces" flicker once more, children abandoned by their caregivers for the sake of the kingdom, in Mark 10:28–30 (Matt 19:27–30; Luke 18:28–30). "Look, we have left everything (πάντα) and followed you," Peter tells Jesus, and in a brief moment, Jesus betrays to the reader what they have left—their families and households, including τέκνα (Mark 10:29; Matt 19:29a; Luke 18:29).[41] Not to worry, however, because the Synoptic Jesus assures followers they will receive fictive children in their new roles as kingdom members. Meanwhile, the "real" children of

---

daughters, prophetesses at Hierapolis in Asia. This he links to a description in Acts (21:8–9) of four unmarried daughters of one "Philip the evangelist" who was "one of the seven." Whether this is a reference to one of the original Twelve, the early Church seems to have believed this apostle had daughters who were firmly committed to an ascetic, thereby *childless*, strain of Christianity.

38. Atkins, *Reading Deconstruction*, 20.

39. Ibid., 20–29.

40. Luke uses this term, meaning "children," whereas Matthew reads υἱὸν ἢ θυγατέρα.

41. Once again, only Luke adds "wife."

the disciples appear no more, neglected by Jesus and the authors for the remainder of the narratives.

A number of years ago, David Sim raised the issue of the plight of the families of the Twelve. Postulating from social-scientific and literary data, Sim thinks it highly probable that the majority of the disciples had wives and children. Working with probabilities, he figures that most of the Twelve were no older than Jesus, and assuming a low figure of two children for a married man between twenty to thirty years of age, one could reasonably project more than twenty children just for the Twelve, in all likelihood "minors and dependants who would have relied upon their fathers for their welfare and security."[42] This is a cost even Jesus does not bear in the narratives. Regarding the cost to the families involved, Sim writes: "We can only imagine that their response to their desertion and rejection involved a mixture of shock, disbelief, anxiety, anger and disapproval." And although instances such as the healing of Peter's mother-in-law could have left positive impressions in Peter's family,

> The probability is that most of the disciples' families would have disapproved strongly of the loss of their husbands and fathers, and suffered considerable anxiety and emotional trauma as a result of their rejection by them. But apart from the emotional effects on their wives and children, the departure of the disciples also had certain economic implications which were probably more serious.[43]

While Sim admittedly relies on inferences and speculation about actual historical figures, I am only making interpretative claims at the literary level, which is certainly informed by cultural standards and the feasibility of social action in the authors' era. Nevertheless, because the Synoptic authors fail to obscure fully the families of the Twelve, Sim's guiding question and speculations prove useful literary-critical tools for the deconstructive reading undertaken here. Despite their apparent attention to children in some narrative scenes, we might seriously begin to wonder whether the Synoptic authors and the Jesus therein really cared all that much for "real" children.

42. Sim, "What about the Wives and Children," 380–81.
43. Ibid., 382–83.

Leaving Children Behind: the Healing Narratives

Returning to our three Synoptic healing stories, the parents seem quite concerned for their children. They go to lengths to gain Jesus' attention and believe he can do something to restore the children to them. The Synoptic authors seem concerned to portray these incidents surrounding children. In each gospel, their restorations function as one of the signs of the apocalypse of the kingdom of God. Furthermore, despite the fact that they are mere children, they are among the socially marginal frequently juxtaposed against the religious elite and the Twelve, the lowly for whom Jesus displays particular concern, —or does he?

Previously, I recounted the staccato-like movement of Jesus in Mark as we approached the healing narrative of Jairus' daughter (Mark 5:21–24, 35–43; Matt 9:18–19, 23–26; Luke 8:40–42, 49–56). He and his earliest followers go throughout Galilee, not only healing and exorcising demons, but, as we have seen, he also trades his biological family for a fictive one based on discipleship. Then, we reenter the first child healing.

> And one of the synagogue rulers, named Jairus, came and seeing Jesus, fell at his feet, and repeatedly begged him saying, "My little daughter is near death (ἐσχάτως ἔχει). Come and lay your hands on her in order that she may be healed (σωθῇ) and live." (Mark 5:22–23)

Reading for children, we notice the young daughter is nameless; her identity as an individual is unimportant to the Synoptic authors. It is lost in the identity of her father, the synagogue leader, and, for Mark and Luke, in her emerging sexuality (as a girl of twelve; Mark 5:42; Luke 8:42). Furthermore, although I raised several questions in the previous chapter about her relationship with her parents, what of the source of her trouble? Does she suffer from an ailment or a mortal accident of some sort? The interpolation of the woman with an issue of blood fosters the notion that the young girl also suffers from some ailment, but the narrative does not say so. Could it have been child abuse, a poorly directed backhand—a reprimand gone wrong? Although she is already dead in Matthew (9:18), none of the authors concern themselves with the cause. True, her father seems desperate, and is drawn to seek Jesus for help. Yet with utter frustration, from the perspective of the one facing death, or that of her caregiver, Jesus does not rush to her, but lets the young girl's life get "interrupted" by a seemingly less pressing problem than death (Mark 5:25–34 and par.).

There is also a great deal of ambiguity involved with a few terms above. The adverbial phrase ἐσχάτως ἔχει (only in Mark and Luke) is typically translated "she is near death" but could also be translated "at her worst," "on the edge of the end," or "at her last." However, ἐσχάτως also conjures larger theological notions in the Synoptics tied to the end of days through the nominative form ἐσχάτον. The use of σωθῇ complicates matters further. A double entendre, it can be translated "she might be healed,"[44] "she might be rescued from harm,"[45] or "she might be saved" in an eternal, divine sense.[46] Are the Synoptic authors concerned about the young girl's temporal life, her eternal existence, or both?

Then, mention of the girl's death and Jesus' response to her father, "μὴ φοβοῦ, μόνον πίστευε" (Mark 5:36; Luke 8:50; omitted in Matthew), alerts the reader to the themes of faith and the power of the dawning kingdom. In the only instance in which Jesus is actually portrayed speaking to a child, he arrives, takes her by the hand, tells her to arise, and she is restored to her parents (Mark 5:41–43 and par). Nevertheless, nothing is required of the nameless girl to receive this gift of life restored. She does not become a follower of Jesus, nor apparently does her father. Although the Synoptic authors seem implicitly to associate this father and daughter with the apocalypse of the kingdom, nothing in the text explicitly reveals they join the sect.[47] Jesus and his band of eschatological followers move on.

Similarly, no name is given to the daughter of the Syrophoenician woman. She lies in bed, afflicted by possession (Mark 7:25–30; Matt 15:22–28). As mentioned earlier, the girl is probably of no help to her mother. An only child, the circumstances of the two do not concern our authors other than their signification of the apocalypse of the kingdom. On the

44. Cf. Mark 6:56.

45. Cf. Matt 14:30.

46. Cf. 1 Cor 1:21; 9:22; Matt 18:11; Mark 16:16.

47. The same holds true for the next two healing narratives examined. As for this one, the phrase μόνον πίστευε in Mark and Luke is very ambiguous and abstract. In the immediate context, Jairus is not told to believe *in Jesus*. The unstated object could be the God of Israel and his power, or simply the power of Jesus as one like Elijah. It does not on its own require a Christological confession. Betsworth argues that, in Mark, this daughter and her parents become part of Jesus' new fictive family because: (1) the actions of teaching, healing, and expressions of compassion by Jesus for marginal characters are associated with the in-breaking of the kingdom; (2) the girl's healing anticipates Jesus' resurrection; and (3) from the faith of the woman with an issue of blood, which interrupts the present healing, it follows that Jairus' shares a similar faith (Betsworth, *The Reign of God*, 113).

one hand, scholars concerned to show Jesus' concern and compassion for children highlight his exorcism of such a marginal figure; after all, the girl is a child, female, and a Gentile.[48] On the other hand, Jesus does not even go to the young girl, touch her, look into her eyes, or exhibit concern for her well-being. The girl does not get to speak. She exhibits no faith. She has no history, nor any future in relation to Jesus or his followers. Instead, he leaves her and her mother for the Sea of Galilee near the Decapolis. At least now the daughter can help her mother until the former marries. Will their fortunes rise or fall? We do not know, for our authors leave them too. Jesus goes on to miraculously feed five thousand (Mark 6:30–44; four thousand in Matt 15:32–38) and have his "glory" revealed in the Transfiguration (Mark 9:2; Matt 17:1–2).

In the third and final child restoration pericope shared among the Synoptics we found another παιδίον suffering from possession (Mark 9:14–29; Matt 17:14–21; Luke 9:37–43a). Again, we child theologians find comfort in Jesus' concern for the boy who, it is emphasized, has been possessed since childhood (Mark 9:21). This time, he faces the child. He casts out the demon, takes the boy by the hand, and restores him to his father (Mark 9:25–27). He is present with the child, and touches him, showing compassion for the most lowly and helpless.

Yet, we are troubled. Does Jesus really care about the child? In Mark, he acts only once the author mentions that he saw a crowd quickly assembling together (9:25).[49] Furthermore, the plight of the boy gets subsumed by the themes of the disciples' lack of faith, the father's belief that there is hope for his son, and the appended comments about the power of prayer (Mark 9:29) or faith (Matt 17:20–21). The boy is restored to his father, but there is no indication they become followers of Jesus, who "went on from there and passed through Galilee," teaching his disciples privately about the resurrection (Mark 9:30).[50] Although they may help the Synoptic authors point toward the eschatological kingdom of Jesus' and his band of follow-

48. Betsworth, "Reign of God is of Such as These," 9–12; *Reign of God*, 127–35; Gundry, "Children," 148–54.

49. This is an interesting inclusion since Mark has already mentioned they were in the midst of a crowd (9:14–17). Likewise, a crowd is present in Matthew (17:14) and Luke (9:37).

50. Matthew tells us Jesus and the disciples went on to a home in Capernaum (17:24; Peter's?), whereas Luke is less specific here about movement. They have been among "the villages" of Galilee (9:1), at Bethsaida for the multiplication of loaves and fish (9:10–17), and then on a mountain for the Transfiguration (9:28–36).

ers, these two figures seem, like Jairus' family, to remain firmly within non-Christian Judaism.

We could argue that in these three pericopae Jesus restores "play" (παίζω/παῖς) to adults who have become separated from play. However, reading Zechariah 8 alongside these stories of children, which describes God's imminent, promised return to Zion, suggests the artificiality of these narratives: "So says the Lord of hosts . . . the streets of [Jerusalem] will be full of boys and girls playing (παιζόντων) in the streets" (8:4–5; LXX). On the one hand, these narratives initiate the characterization of children/play into the social world of the adult protagonist and his movement on the way toward their final destination in Jerusalem. On the other hand, it may be that the Synoptic authors are less interested in actual children and their relationship with discipleship and the kingdom of God, but have incorporated them as a literary motif signaling the identification of Jesus with the in-breaking of God's kingdom. The restorations of playfulness to adult caregivers are perhaps symbolic depictions of the restoration of playfulness among God's people, spilling over into surrounding regions as well. However, in the end, Jesus leaves "play" behind in all three pericopae, and "play" does not follow. He leaves each child and caregiver behind; they are of no further concern to the protagonist or authors.

In other words, if we take seriously the demands and needs of children, there seems a great disconnect between the Synoptic claims of child inclusion and the itinerant nature of Jesus' eschatological gathering of followers. Can we envision any of the children brought to Jesus leaving their fathers and mothers and assuming a life of discipleship? What problems might arise if they do? Our assessment of childhood in the Jewish and Hellenistic-Roman worlds showed that young children were wholly dependent on adults for shelter, food, protection, affection, education or training, and socialization, all of which seems to have taken place in some form of structured environment, i.e., a household, apprenticeship, etc, even if a slave. In the highly patriarchal father-son, master-slave structure of antiquity, children had little or no agency. They did not function autonomously in ancient society. Nor, it seems, could they be envisioned donning the life of a Cynic, a Cynic's pupil, or child. Criticizing Cynics for their detachment from traditional social obligations, the Stoic Epictetus raised the issue of parenting and the needs of children:

> Doesn't one have to provide cloaks for his children? Doesn't he have to send them to school with tablets, writing tools, notebooks?

Doesn't he have to turn down their beds? They can't be Cynics as they come from the womb. If he does not do these things, it would be better to throw them out (ῥῖψαι) than to kill them [i.e., thus be neglected].[51]

Even when a child was exposed or abandoned by pagan, Jewish, or Christian parents, it would stretch the imagination to envision a youngster, like a young Huck Finn, forging autonomous adventures. There is simply a lack of evidence to suggest that non-adult children were part of any itinerating movement elsewhere, which brings the plausibility of the Synoptic author's depiction into question. Despite the fact that they frequently portray Jesus bringing healing to households and restoring children to their parents, they have not obscured the fact that becoming a disciple involves a lifestyle almost necessitating estrangement from real families for participation in the mission of evangelization.

Reading for Children—Themes of Abandonment in the Passion

Jesus, the Abandoned Teacher and Son

A final problem with Synoptic claims of inclusiveness toward children may be found by some readers in the theme of abandonment. Is not Jesus abandoned by his closest disciples from Gethsemane forward?[52] In fact, the entire passion, particularly in Mark and Matthew, is overshadowed by the theme of abandonment.[53] As we have seen, the Synoptic authors certainly suggest many followers have abandoned their family ties for the sake of the kingdom (Mark 10:28 and par.). For Jesus, not even family or children must supersede one's allegiance to him.

Once in Judea, the plot of the passion begins to unfold. After celebrating the final symbolic meal together, Jesus and his closest followers go over to the Mount of Olives, where he tells them they will all fall away (σκανδαλισθήσεσθε) because of him before the night ends. Then Mark and

51. Epictetus, *Diatr.* 3.22.74, quoted in Boswell, *Kindness*, 86.

52. See Mark 14:32–15:41 and parallels, except for the women who are at *some distance* from the cross.

53. The theme of divine abandonment does not carry forward in Luke as it does in Mark and Matthew, where angels are sent to attend Jesus in Gethsemane at the advent of his hour, and Jesus is never without control as he dies on the cross (Luke 23:46).

Matthew appropriate Zechariah 13:7 for the occasion, where the shepherd is struck and the sheep will be scattered (διασκορπισθήσονται).[54]

Quickly, we are told the disciples "abandon" (ἀφέντες) Jesus at his arrest and flee (Mark 14:50; Matt 26:46). In Mark, a young man who had also been following Jesus "abandons" (καταλιπὼν) his linen garment, and flees naked.[55] As the reader proceeds through the "trial" accounts, we arrive at Peter's denial where he thrice denies he knew the one he had left all to follow. The scene underscores the depth of his abandonment of Jesus at this point, and probably is representative of the abandonment of Jesus by all of the disciples who went to Jerusalem, or at least the Twelve (Mark 14:53–65; Matt 26:57–68; Luke 22:54–71). But, it is through deconstruction's attention to "otherness," to ambiguous words or characterizations, that we are able to view with an ironic twist how Peter's denials are brought to the fore by a servant girl (παιδίσκη), who confronts him in the courtyard of the high priest (Mark 14:66–69; Matt 26:69–72; Luke 22:56).

The context in Matthew and Mark is ambiguous enough. Peter is alone in the darkness and cold of night, which contrasts with the constant kinship, warmth, and light that characterized the movement throughout earlier portions of the narratives. Suddenly, the adult male follower is confronted by a shadowy figure. The face of female servant, or a young girl, flickers in firelight where Peter warms himself.[56] Clearly we can interpret her as young girl whom for once the gospels grant a degree of authority. Empowered with a voice of her own, she stands there, calling out one who has abandoned Jesus. However, the fire fades and flickers, and with every ember cast up, the image seems unstable; for, the young girl/female servant may also be an apparition, a haunting metaphor for the children whom the adult disciples would have denied being brought to Jesus.

Yet, it is not just his followers who abandon Jesus in Mark and Matthew. In another ironic twist, these authors place a cry of neglect on Jesus

54. Mark 14:27; Matt 26:31. Two verses later, Peter makes his claim that he will not fall away, even though the others will, and then Jesus prophesies his treble denial.

55. ἀφέντες, from ἀφίημι, in this instance also meaning to leave behind, neglect, forsake (Newman, "ἀφίημι," 29); καταλείπω, also meaning abandon, leave behind, neglect, forsake (Newman, "καταλείπω," 94).

56. Of diminutive form, παιδίσκη can simply mean a "young girl," or "a young female slave," but some degree of youth is implied, however we take the term (LS, "παιδίσκη," 512). As mentioned in footnote 49 in chapter one, Matthew has two παιδισκῶν accuse Peter in the courtyard, whereas Mark is more ambiguous about whether one or two maids confront him. Luke tries to negate the non-adult status of παιδίσκη in 22:56 by the reply of Peter in v. 57, "I don't know him, γύναι."

lips on the cross, abandonment by the divine Father (Mark 15:34; Matt 27:46): "ὁ θεός μου ὁ θεός μου, εἰς τί ἐγκατέλιπές με." In this quote from Psalm 22:1, ἐγκατέλιπές is the second aorist, second person, singular form of ἐγκαταλείπω, meaning "you have left behind," "abandoned," "neglected," or "forsaken."[57] At the climax of their respective narratives, the divine child of heaven issues a cry of abandonment by his fictive Father, who did not protect his son from death. Finally, the centurion solidifies the image of child abandonment by his confession that the crucified was a son of God (Mark 15:39; Matt 27:54; cf. Mark 1:11).

Children and Followers Abandoned by Jesus

In light of the many cases of child abuse emerging from the shadows of the modern Church, a place where children are taught to seek divine protection and care, and with the theme of abandonment so prevalent, I think it highly probable that victims of abuse within the Church often ask, "Where was God?" The sense of divine abandonment can potentially overwhelm one's faith, causing one to "fall away." At this point, I think it appropriate ask whether the character of Jesus abandons children in the Synoptic Gospels.

At the outset of the movement, Jesus and his disciples are depicted as a group largely on the move throughout Galilee, Judea, and surrounding regions, proclaiming the message of the apocalypse of the kingdom of God. In the process, a new fictive family is created by the calling of individuals to an allegiance to Jesus. In *Discipleship and Family Ties*, Barton notes: "It is noteworthy . . . that the disciples' renunciation of their household ties, in [Mark] 1.16–20, corresponds with the mission instruction to renounce possessions and depend upon the hospitality of others in 6.7–13."[58] In other words, an operative point within the narratives is that the calling is to individuals, *not households or family units*, to divest themselves of all typical earthly ties, including one's family, in order to *follow* Jesus (Mark 13:10).[59]Therefore, along the way, traditional family ties are relativized by both Jesus and his followers in favor of this new fictive eschatological family. Soon, however, the authors begin to provide ominous signs about this charismatic figure.

---

57. Newman, "ἐγκαταλείπω," 51.

58. Barton, *Discipleship and Family Ties*, 63–64.

59. Ibid., 64.

Even in Galilee, the Synoptic authors present Jesus disclosing his pre-determined passion (Mark 8:31–33; Matt 16:21–23; Luke 9:22). Just after exorcising the boy with the demon, he foretells his passion a second time (Mark 9:30–32; Matt 17:22–23; Luke 9:43b–45). Immediately thereafter, we find the disciples' dispute over greatness in the kingdom, and Jesus' placing a child in their midst. Not far removed, he receives children brought to him, raises them up in his arms, and blesses them; again, if we take Derrett and Gundy's interpretation, he even assumes a parental role by adopting them. Then, having seemingly centered children within the kingdom and its demands of discipleship, he proceeds to explain to them the exceeding cost of discipleship. Immediately, they are "on the way" to Jerusalem, and he describes for a third time his unavoidable martyrdom (Mark 10:32–34; Matt 20:17–19; Luke 18:31–34).[60] Although the disciples typically fail to grasp what these predictions imply, the reader does not. Together, these disclosures foretell a difficult and confusing reality for characters in the narrative. This charismatic leader will intentionally leave behind his new fictive family.

If we follow the interpretation that Jesus "adopts" children into his new eschatological family, but the children cannot "follow," or acquiesce, or have agency, and then Jesus leaves, goes off, moves on itinerating, then is he abandoning them? Jesus (and the Synoptic authors) may understand his actions as symbolic or eschatological, but can non-adult children in the narratives understand him this way?[61] If the call to discipleship leads to tragic family ruptures, where perhaps one parent joins the movement and another not, does this do a temporal disservice to children? Suppose Jesus "adopts" a child brought to him, and its parents subsequently choose not to follow, but to remain steadfastly within non-Christian Judaism. Has he abandoned the child if he moves on?

Finally, imagine for a moment that a few children can decide to uproot and follow Jesus in the Synoptic narratives; Huck floats down the Jordan with other members of Jesus' eschatological family toward Jerusalem. What impressions are made on "adopted children" when their adopter divests himself of all earthly inheritance and then abandons them for death on a Roman cross? There are no children depicted with the women "gazing from

---

60. Matthew briefly conveys a fourth passion prediction in 26:1–2.

61. Remember that in Mark, even members of the Twelve often fail to understand Jesus' teaching. The presumption among Greco-Roman authors as well as Paul was that young children lacked the reasoning ability of adults.

afar" at Jesus on the cross (Matt 27:55–56; Mark 15:40–41; Luke 23:49), at the tomb, or for the resurrection appearances. Instead, we must go back in the courtyard of the high priest to find the last character of a child in the Synoptics.[62] It is our apparition, the face of the servant girl challenging Peter, haunting the story from the firelight (Mark 14:66–69 and par.). For this somewhat amorphous παιδίσκη conveys within her not only the suggestion of a young girl and/or a servant girl, but notions of jest and mockery. Unlike Jesus' adult followers who meet him in Galilee or Jerusalem, this collective representation of "real" children resolutely stands within the courtyard of the high priest,[63] the chief opponent of Jesus in the end, still in non-Christian Judaism, in some sense mocking the one who left the "real" children of the narratives for martyrdom, a witness against those who abandon.

62. In Mark, the lone figure in the empty tomb (16:5) is a νεανίσκος, meaning "a youth, young man" (LS, "νεανίσκος," 459), making his identification more ambiguous than Matthew's "angel of the Lord" (28:2) and Luke's "ἄνδρες δύο" (24:4). However, the description of his apparel and the women's amazement suggest the figure is more a part of the resurrected world than the temporal. The figure is often connected or contrasted with the young man in Mark 14:51 who flees naked from Jesus arrest, or read as an angel (Donahue and Harrington, *Mark*, 458; Perkins, *Mark*, 730–31; Mann, *Mark*, 1080); see also MacDonald, *Homeric Epics*, 162–65 who views the role of the young man as that of an oracle, implicitly warning Jesus' followers to flee Jerusalem in lieu of its coming destruction for rejecting him.

63. Ironically, the courtyard acts as a liminal space between the sanctuary of the house and the outside world.

CHAPTER FIVE

ECHOES OF NEGLECT

> Jesus, Friend of little children; Be a friend to me;
> Take my hand, and ever keep me, close to Thee.
>
> Never leave me, nor forsake me; Ever be my friend;
> For I need Thee, from life's dawning to its end.[1]

EACH YEAR FOR OVER the past ten years, the National Child Abuse and Neglect Data System for the US has substantiated well over 800,000 cases of reported abuse and neglect of children. As of the 2005 report, nearly 80 percent of perpetrators were parents, while nearly 7 percent were other relatives. Disabled or chronically ill children are twice as likely to be abuse or neglected. Of the total number of cases substantiated as of 2005, neglect accounted for 62.8 percent, physical abuse 16.6 percent, sexual abuse 9.3 percent, emotional/psychological abuse 7.1 percent, medical neglect two percent, and among the category of "other," which registers at 14.3 percent is abandonment.[2] UNICEF reports that as many as 1.2 million children world-wide could be victims of human trafficking.[3]

In lieu of such terrible statistics, one would hope that institutions of faith, representatives of the divine in the tumultuous sea of humanity stand out as a beacon of hope and healing for such children. Often they do. Unfortunately, however, churches and families of faith have also sometimes

---

1. Lyrics by Walter J. Mathams (1853–1931), public domain.

2. American Humane Association, "Child Abuse and Neglect Statistics," lines 14–39.

3. UNICEF, "Child Trafficking," lines 7–9.

been the venue for child endangerment, abuse, or neglect. In recent years, cases of reported sexual abuse of children by Catholic priests have been the focus of intense media attention, and millions of dollars have been paid out in damages to the victims of abuse. However, in terms of the raw numbers, Protestant churches receive the vast majority of sexual abuse allegations every year.[4] As I mentioned in the introduction, I too became aware of an incident in my childhood church.

What happens to children when their faith fails them, when the people they look up to for guidance, nurturance, protection, and faith are neglectful, or worse? How do victims of childhood abuse negotiate questions of faith when prayerful petitions are met with absolute silence? As one popular author asks, "Where is God when it hurts?"[5] A related question upon which this study rests is, of course, what does it look like to find instances of abuse or neglect in the Bible? In the Synoptics for instance, what problems might have arisen if some children had taken Jesus seriously and become disciples in this eschatological band? Can we reasonably project the impact on children who had one or both parents leave their possessions to follow Jesus? In short, the Synoptic authors, in conjuring the picture they do, literally did not seem to have considered the complexities of children as social equals in the kingdom.

I have not intended to bring resolution to a problematic reading. Rather, I have intended to raise a problematic reading from the shadows, to expose a reading for further examination and scrutiny. For most Christians, the Jesus of the Gospels is interpreted as the paradigmatic healer and comforter; he walks with his followers and converses with them along their journey. However, the texts presented by the Synoptic authors are not bound by a monolithic interpretation, and every reader brings something a little different to the text as he or she reads it.

With this in mind, I offer in conclusion a couple of brief imaginative literary [re]constructions of children in relation to the eschatological movement of Jesus and his followers. My hope is that the theological reflection it is meant to stir will provide further impetus on the multivocality of texts and the presence of children within texts.

4. Clayton, "Sex Abuse."
5. Yancey, *Where is God?*

Let the Little Children Come: A Reading for Reflection

Amidst the setting of Mark 10:15 (Matt 18:3; Luke 18:17), there are a couple of young children; let us say a brother and sister, at a home in the region of "Judea, beyond the Jordan" (Mark 10:1). It is mid morning. She has been drawing water; he has been removing stones from the field, an annual spring chore. They hear voices at the house in the distance, and their master directing their mother to fetch his daughters for a brief midday trip. The boy arches his back and reaches for another small stone protruding from the dusty soil and places it in his collecting basket. There is no special visitor today for these young slaves or their mother.[6]

Meanwhile, the two young daughters accompany their father and mother to see these travelers come down from Galilee. Perhaps they have heard him speak of this teacher and his band before; perhaps not. Along the road a handful of other children emerge alongside their caregivers, some carrying infants,[7] and soon they make their way into the audience of Jesus and his eschatological band. We do not know why, but adults begin bringing children up to this holy man or teacher, and a confrontation between them and the disciples is quickly dealt with—the teacher is willing to receive the children brought to him (Mark 10:13–14b and par.).

For the young girls, they remember nothing similar ever. Sheltered by their father, they are nearly always confined to home, and the spatial limitations of Jewish women. They are never in the company of complete male strangers. Now they are led by the hand of their father past the gaze of followers and up to this strange man who tells the crowd, "the kingdom of God consists of such like these" (Mark 14c). Then he tells the adults, "Truly I tell you, whoever does not welcome the kingdom of God like a young

---

6. Although the Synoptic Jesus presents a high view of service to others, particularly in Mark (recall this theme in Mark 9:33–37), nowhere is a servant brought to Jesus for healing. In Matthew 8:5–13 (and par.), the παῖς of the centurion could be read as "boy," but is nearly always taken to be a *servant* boy (see Albright and Mann, *Matthew*, 93), perhaps because Luke uses the term δοῦλος (Luke 7:2). John complicates matters further by making the person a son of the centurion (John 4:46b–54). Although the Matthean reference could be taken as a "boy," to do so would merely further marginalize the probable slave, effectively erasing this social figure in favor of a non-slave child. Meanwhile, the centurion's "servant" is not brought to Jesus, and Jesus is not taken to this figure. While the centurion's faith is typically credited as the reason the child need not be present, the servile status of the character is also a reasonable interpretation.

7. Recall that Luke uses the term βρέφη here (18:15).

child will never enter it" (v.15). The older girl ponders what he means. Have they ever welcomed God's kingdom? If yes, in what way have they done so?

Problems spring to mind for the interpreter. Given what we know today about child development and education, how do the ages of the children shape their responses? Do they, as we so often imagine, reciprocate the supposed warmth and acceptance extended by Jesus? Do they tremble in fear with downcast eyes, avoiding all eye contact with these unfamiliar adult males, as one might culturally expect? If we consider them infants to toddlers, there is presumably little or no cognitive or linguistic response. If we entertain an older child, such as the older of our two representative daughters, she might think to herself: what did he mean about *entering* God's kingdom, and what have I done that adults would look to me? Yet, despite these musings, the Synoptic authors do not entertain the thought or spoken world of children here. At this point, the insight of William Strange cannot be understated.

> Although Jesus welcomed children, commended them as examples and spoke of them as objects of care, we find in the gospels that he never actually spoke *to* them. Apart from two words of healing to Jairus' daughter (Mk 5:41), none of the gospel writers record any saying of Jesus spoken to a child, nor any teaching directed at children as a group.[8]

Whatever this teacher was talking about, perhaps their father will explain it later. I imagine an elderly man in the crowd who suddenly repeats a scripture in a hushed voice: "Behold, I and the children that the Lord has given to me are signs and omens in Israel" (Isa 8:18). It seems odd that Jesus speaks highly of them as children, but he is clearly talking to the adults. After the protagonist finishes touching the children, Matthew simply states "he went away" (19:15). Meanwhile, the slave girl and her mother almost have the meals prepared when the daughters return home with the master.

The Cost of Discipleship: A Reading for Reflection

Elias Barjacob heaves with all his might on the net of fish to hoist it into the boat. His small palms ooze blood against the waterlogged bandages encircling them, as the coarse fishnet slowly slips against the flesh and bandages. He wrestles the net with his older cousins and his grandfather. Perhaps,

---

8. Strange, *Children*, 62.

rather than the net's tireless effort to callous the young boy's hands, it is the constant degradation of his father and uncle by his grandfather, Zebedee, that irritates the emotional wound opened by the absence of his father. None of the other boys his age work the nets, but with his father parading around with some "teacher," his grandfather said he had little choice.

His grandfather is not the only voice impacted by his father's absence, for the voices of his mother and her father are full of questions, uncertainty, anger, and fear as they bear the disgrace not unnoticed by the wider community. His mother shouts in anger as his grandmother kneads dough for the evening meal, "Our store reserves are dwindling. We owe taxes and have mouths to feed, now. Abraham left the home of his ancestors and followed God, not some person from a town like Nazareth. He had a destination. He did not wander from place to place living off of the hospitality of others so that he could listen to someone talk about the things of God." What will the boy come to think of his father? What will he think of the character of Jesus?

Conclusion

In this project I have raised problematic issues involved with the characterization of Jesus as child-friendly in the Synoptic Gospels. In doing so, we have seen that the inclusion of children in the kingdom of God within the Synoptic narratives is not unproblematic, but is tempered by images of household disruption and the alienation of children as a consequence of Jesus' eschatological gathering of followers. There is a lack of congruence between the social world conjured by the authors in the Synoptic narratives, and the social *realia* of the day regarding children, bringing their depictions of child inclusivity into question.

As scholars who want to foreground "real" children in narratives, it seems we are faced with a stark choice in the Synoptic Gospels. On the one hand, we can follow where the Synoptic authors want to lead us. It is on a journey toward an eschatological kingdom, where the humble are exalted, and the exalted brought low. It is where the religiously superior are spiritually inferior, where the socially and ritually marginal peoples of this world, including children, enjoy a new status of greatness. By becoming a disciple of Jesus, characters begin to enter into this kingdom; they begin to see its benefits. Crowds of hungry are miraculously fed. Mere fishermen become important, entrusted with the secrets of the kingdom. Sinners are forgiven outside the confines of the temple and ritual sacrifice. Women actively engage as disciples, following even to the cross, while children are attended to, received as God himself, and positioned as central to this eschatological kingdom. At last, Jesus secures for all in his new fictive family an eternal inheritance in their new kingdom through his passion and resurrection.

And behold, the eschatological vision laid down by the prophets includes children! Zechariah foretells a day when children will freely play in the streets of Jerusalem (8:5). In Isaiah's vision of the new heavens and earth, God promises that infants will forever live beyond a few days, never to be cut short again (65:20). The asp or adder will never again harm or take the life of infants and toddlers (11:8). No one will bear children only to see them suffer (11:62). "A child will lead the calf and lion together" without fear (11:62), and if one could die at the age of a hundred, she would seem a mere youth (65:20). Perhaps these are the visions of children the Synoptic authors place before the disciples when Jesus promises a hundredfold children in return for the ones they left behind (Mark 10:30; Matt 19:28).

On the other hand, for the interpreter who takes seriously the plight of "real" children in the temporal world of the text, he or she must deliberately separate the plight of temporal families from the eschatological promises of the authors. One must refuse to sacrifice real children for eschatological or metaphorical ones in the narratives.

BIBLIOGRAPHY

Aasgaard, Reidar. "Children in Anitquity and Early Christianity: Research History and Central Issues." *Familia* 33 (2006) 23–46.

Aland, B., et al., editorss. *Novum Testamentum Graece*. 27th ed. Stuttgart: Deutsche Bibelgesellschaft, 1993.

Albright, William F., and C.S. Mann. *Matthew*. 1st ed. Anchor Bible 26. Garden City, NY: Doubleday, 1971.

American Humane Association. "Child Abuse and Neglect Statistics." Online: http:// www.americanhumane.org/children/stop-child-abuse/fact-sheets/child-abuse-and-neglect-statistics.html.

Ariès, Philippe. *Centuries of Childhood: A Social History of Family Life*. Translated by R. Baldiek. New York: Vintage, 1962. Originally published as *L'enfant et la vie familiale sous l'ancien régime*. Paris: Plon, 1960.

Aristophanes. Translated by Benjamin Bickley Rogers. *Clouds*. 3 vols. LCL. Cambridge, MA: Harvard University Press, 1974–1990.

Aristotle in Twenty-Three Volumes. Vol. 19, *The Nicomachean Ethics*. Tanslated by H. Rackham. LCL. Cambridge, MA: Harvard University Press, 1975.

Baer, David. "Near the Cross." *Generations Newsletter* 3/1 (2004) 3. Online: https://www. familiesalive.org/wp-content/uploads/2013/05/Generations-Vol-3-Issue-1.pdf.

Bailey, James L. "Experiencing the Kingdom of God as a Little Child: A Rereading of Mark 10:13–16." *Word and World* 15 (1995) 58–67.

Bakke, Odd Magne. *When Children Became People: The Birth of Childhood in Early Christianity*. Translated by B. McNeil. Minneapolis: Fortress, 2005.

Balla, Peter. *The Child-Parent Relationship in the New Testament and Its Environment*. WUNT zum NT. Tübingen: Mohr/Siebeck, 2003.

Balswick, Jack O., and Judith K. Balswick. *The Family: A Christian Perspective on the Contemporary Home*. 2nd ed. Grand Rapids: Baker, 1999.

Barton, Stephen C. *Discipleship and Family Ties in Matthew and Mark*. Cambridge: Cambridge University Press, 1994.

———. *The Family in Theological Perspective*. Edinburgh: T. & T. Clark, 1996.

———. "Jesus-Friend of Little Children?" In *The Contours of Christian Education*, edited by Jeff Astley and David Day, 30–40. Great Wakering, Essex: McCrimmon, 1992.

Baumgarten, Elisheva. "Judaism." In *Children and Childhood in World Religions: Primary Sources and Texts,* edited by Don S. Browning and Marcia J. Bunge, 15–81. New Brunswick, NJ: Rutgers University Press, 2009.

Beal, Timothy K. "Glossary; Ideology and Intertextuality: Surplus of Meaning and Controlling the Means of Production." In *Reading Between Texts: Intertextuality and the Hebrew Bible*, edited by Danna N. Fewell, 21–39. Louisville: Westminster John Knox, 1992.

Beard, Mary, et al. *Religions of Rome*. 2 vols. Cambridge: Cambridge University Press, 2009.

Beasley-Murray, George R. "Church and Child in the New Testament." *Baptist Quarterly* 21 (1966) 206–18.

Bedouelle, Guy. "Reflection on the Place of the Child in the Church: 'Suffer the Little Children to Come Unto Me.'" *Communio* 12 (1985) 349–67.

Best, Ernest. *Disciples and Discipleship: Studies in the Gospel According to St. Mark*, edited by Ernest Best. Edinburgh: T. & T. Clark, 1986.

Betsworth, Sharon. "The Child and Jesus in the Gospel of Matthew." *Journal of Childhood and Religion* 1/4 (2010) 1–14.

———. "The Reign of God is of Such as These: Children in the Gospel of Mark." Paper presented at the annual meeting of the Society of Biblical Literature, Boston, MA, November, 2008.

———. *The Reign of God is Such as These: A Socio-Literary Analysis of Daughters in the Gospel of Mark*. New York: T. & T. Clark, 2010.

Bible and Culture Collective. *The Postmodern Bible*. New Haven: Yale University Press, 1995.

Black, Matthew. "The Markan Parable of the Child in the Midst." *Expository Times* 59 (1947–1948) 14–16.

Boadt, Lawrence. "The Child in the Bible." *The Bible Today* 103 (1979) 2082–88.

Boring, M. Eugene. *The Gospel of Matthew*. New Interpreter's Bible 8. Nashville: Abingdon, 1995.

Boswell, John. "Exposition and *Oblatio*: The Abandonment of Children and the Ancient and Medieval Family." *American Historical Review* 89 (1984) 10–33

———. *The Kindness of Strangers: The Abandonment of Children in Western Europe from Late Antiquity to the Renaissance*. Chicago: University of Chicago Press, 1988.

Bradley, Keith R. *Discovering the Roman Family: Studies in Roman Social History*. New York: Oxford University Press, 1991.

———. "Wet-nursing at Rome: A Study in Social Relations." In *The Family in Ancient Rome: New Perspectives*, edited by Beryl Rawson, 201–29. Ithaca: Cornell University Press, 1986.

Brown, Francis, et al. *The New Brown, Driver, Briggs Hebrew and English Lexicon of the Old Testament*. Lafayette, IN: Associated, 1981.

Brown, Peter. "Bodies and Minds: Sexuality and Renunciation in Early Christianity." In *Sexualities in History: A Reader*, edited by Kim M. Phillips and Barry Reay, 129–39. New York: Routledge, 2001.

———. *The Body and Society: Men, Women, and Sexual Renunciation in Early Christianity*. New York: Columbia University Press, 1988.

Browning, Don S., et al. *From Culture Wars to Common Ground: Religion and the American Family Debate*. 1st ed. Family, Religion, and Culture. Louisville: Westminster John Knox, 1997.

Browning, Don S., and Marcia J. Bunge, editors. *Children and Childhood in World Religions: Primary Sources and Texts*. Rutgers Series in Childhood Studies. New Brunswick, NJ: Rutgers University Press, 2009.

Browning, Don S., and Bonnie J. Miller-McLemore, editors. *Children and Childhood in American Religions*. Rutgers Series in Childhood Studies. New Brunswick, NJ: Rutgers University Press, 2009.

Brueggemann, Walter. "Vulnerable Children, Divine Passion, and Human Obligation." In *The Child in the Bible*, edited by Marcia J. Bunge et al., 399–422. Grand Rapids: Eerdmans, 2008.

Bunge, Marcia J., editor. *The Child in Christian Thought*. Religion, Marriage, and Family. Grand Rapids: Eerdmans, 2001.

Bunge, Marcia J., et al. *The Child in the Bible*. Grand Rapids: Eerdmans, 2008.

Burkert, Walter. *Ancient Mystery Cults*. Cambridge, MA: Harvard University Press, 1987.

———. *Greek Religion*. Translated by John Raffan. Cambridge, MA: Harvard University Press, 1985.

Carroll, John T. "'What Then Will This Child Become?': Perspectives on Children in the Gospel of Luke." In *The Child in the Bible*, edited by Marcia J. Bunge et al., 177–94. Grand Rapids: Eerdmans, 2008.

Carroll, John T. "Children in the Bible." *Interpretation* 55/2 (2001) 121–34.

Carson, Donald A. "Matthew." In *Zondervan NIV Bible Commentary*, edited by Kenneth L. Barker and John R. Kohlenberger, 2:1–135. Grand Rapids: Zondervan, 1994.

Carter, Warren. *Households and Discipleship: A Study of Matthew 19–20*. JSNTSupp 103; Sheffield: JSOT Press, 1994.

Cartlidge, David R., and David L. Dungan, editors. *Documents for the Study of the Gospels*. Rev. ed. Minneapolis: Fortress, 1994.

Cassius, Dio. *Roman History*. Translated by Earnest Cary. 9 vols. LCL. Cambridge, MA: Harvard University Press, 1914–1927.

Charles, Robert Henry, editor. *Pseudepigrapha of the Old Testament*. Bellingham, WA: Logos, 2004.

Charlesworth, James H., editor. *The Pseudepigrapha*. 2 vols. Garden City, NY: Doubleday, 1983, 1985.

Chronica Regiae Coloniensis Continuatio prima, s.a.1213, MGH SS XXIV 17–18. In *The Crusades: A Documentary History*, translated by James Brundage, 213. Milwaukee: Marquette University Press, 1962.

Cicero in Twenty-Eight Volumes. Translated by Walter Miller. LCL. Cambridge, MA: Harvard University Press, 1968.

Clark, Elizabeth A. "Anti-familial Tendencies in Ancient Christianity." *Journal of the History of Sexuality* 5/3 (1995) 356–79.

Clayton, Mark. "Sex Abuse Spans Spectrum of Churches." *Christian Science Monitor*, 5 April 2002. Online: http://www.csmonitor.com/2002/0405/p01s01-ussc.html?sms_ss=email&at_xt=4dboea6dee49bced%2C0.

Clements, Ronald E. "Relation of Children to the People of God in the Old Testament." *Baptist Quarterly* 21 (1966) 195–205.

Cohen, Shaye J. D., editor. *The Jewish Family in Antiquity*. Brown Judaic Studies 289. Atlanta: Scholars, 1993.

Collins, John J. "Marriage, Divorce, and Family in Second Temple Judaism." In *Families in Ancient Israel*, edited by Leo G. Perdue et al., 104–62. Louisville: Westminster John Knox, 1997.

Cooper, John. *The Child in Jewish History*. Northvale, NJ: Aronson, 1996.

Crossan, John Dominic. *The Historical Jesus: The Life of a Jewish Mediterranean Peasant*. San Francisco: HarperSanFrancisco, 1991.

————. *Jesus: A Revolutionary Biography*. New York: HarperSanFrancisco, 1994.

————. "Kingdom and Children: A Study in the Aphoristic Tradition." *Semeia* 29 (1983) 75–96.

Culpepper, R. Alan. *The Gospel of Luke*. New Interpreter's Bible 9. Nashville: Abingdon, 1995.

Derrett, J. Duncan M. "Why Jesus Blessed the Children (Mk 10:13–16 par.)." *Novum Testamentum* 25 (1983) 1–18.

Derrida, Jacques. "Letter to a Japanese Friend." In *Derrida and Différance*, edited by David Wood and Robert Bernasconi, 1–5. Evanston, IL: Northwestern University Press, 1988.

————. *Of Grammatology*. Baltimore: Johns Hopkins University Press, 1997.

deSilva, David A. *Honor, Patronage, Kinship & Purity: Unlocking New Testament Culture*. Downers Grove, IL: InterVarsity, 2000.

Dillon, Matthew. *Girls and Women in Classical Greek Religion*. London: Routledge, 2002.

Diogenes Laertius. *Lives of Eminent Philosophers*. Translated by R. D. Hicks. 2 vols. LCL. Cambridge, MA: Harvard University Press, 1972, 1970.

Dionysius of Halicarnassus. *Roman Antiquities*. 2 vols. LCL. Cambridge, MA: Harvard University Press, 1974.

Dixon, Suzanne. *The Roman Family*. Ancient Society and History. Baltimore: Johns Hopkins University Press, 1992.

————. *Childhood, Class, and Kin in the Roman World*. London: Routledge, 2001.

Donahue, John R., and Daniel J. Harrington. *Gospel of Mark*. Sacra Pagina 2. Collegeville, MN: Liturgical, 2002.

Draper, Jonathan A. "Jesus and the Renewal of Local Community in Galilee: Challenge to a Communitarian Christology." *Journal of Theology for Southern Africa* 87 (1994) 29–42.

Duling, Dennis C. "Kingdom of God, Kingdom of Heaven." In *Anchor Bible Dictionary*, edited by David Noel Freedman, 4:56–59. Garden City, NY: Doubleday, 1992.

du Plessis, Isak. "Discipleship According to Luke's Gospel." *Religion and Theology* 2/1 (1995) 58–71.

Epictetus. *The Discourses as Reported by Arrian, The Manual, and Fragments*. Translated by W. A. Oldfather. 2 vols. LCL Cambridge, MA: Harvard University Press, 1967, 1978.

Ehrman, Bart D., editor. *After the New Testament: A Reader in Early Christianity*. New York: Oxford University Press, 1999.

Eisenbaum, Pamela. *Paul Was Not a Christian: the Original Message of a Misunderstood Apostle*. New York: HarperCollins, 2009.

Eyben, Emiel. "Family Planning in Graeco-Roman Antiquity." *Ancient Society* 11–12 (1980–1981) 5–82.

————. "Fathers and Sons." In *Marriage, Divorce, and Children in Ancient Rome*, edited by Beryl Rawson, 114–43. Canberra: Humanities Research Centre, 1991.

Ferguson, Everett. *Backgrounds of Early Christianity* 2nd Edition. Grand Rapids: Eerdmans, 1993.

Fewell, Danna Nolan. *The Children of Israel: Reading the Bible for the Sake of Our Children*. Nashville: Abingdon, 2003.

————. "Deconstructive Criticism: Achsah and the (E)razed City of Writing." In *Judges and Method*, edited by Gale Yee, 119–45. Minneapolis: Fortress, 1995.

Fewell, Danna Nolan, editor. *Reading Between Texts: Intertextuality and the Hebrew Bible.* Louisville: Westminster John Knox, 1992.

Fewell, Danna Nolan, and David Gunn. *Gender, Power, and Promise: The Subject of the Bible's First Story.* Nashville: Abingdon, 1993.

Fitzmyer, Joseph A. *The Gospel According to Luke.* Anchor Bible 28–28a. Garden City, NY: Doubleday, 1981.

Fowl, Stephen E. "Receiving the Kingdom of God as a Child: Children and Riches in Luke 18:15ff." *New Testament Studies* 39 (1993) 153–58.

Francis, James. "Children and Childhood in the New Testament." In *The Family in Theological Perspective*, edited by Stephen C. Barton, 65–85. Edinburgh: T. & T. Clark, 1996.

Fredriksen, Paula. *Jesus of Nazareth, King of the Jews.* New York: Knopf, 2000.

Fretheim, Terrence E. "God, Abraham, and the Abuse of Isaac." *Word and World* 15/1 (1995) 49-57.

———. "'God Was with the Boy' (Genesis 21:20) Children in the Book of Genesis." In *The Child in the Bible*, edited by Marcia J. Bunge et al., 3–23. Grand Rapids: Eerdmans, 2008.

García Martínez, Florentino, and Eibert J. C. Tigchelaar. *The Dead Sea Scrolls Study Edition.* 2 Vols. Leiden: Brill, 2000.

Gardner, Jane F., and Thomas E. J. Wiedemann, editors. *The Roman Household: a Sourcebook.* London: Routledge, 1991.

The Attic Nights of Aulus Gellius. Vols. 1 and 2. Translated by John C. Rolfe. LCL. Cambridge, MA: Harvard University Press, 1967.

Golden, Mark. "Childhood in Ancient Greece." In *Coming of Age in Ancient Greece: Images of Childhood from the Classical Past*, edited by Jenifer Neils and John H. Oakley, 13–29. New Haven: Yale University Press, 2003.

———. *Children and Childhood in Classical Athens.* Ancient Society and History. Baltimore: Johns Hopkins University Press, 1990.

———. "Demography and the Exposure of Girls at Athens." *Phoenix* 35 (1981) 316–31.

Gopnik, Alison. *The Philosophical Baby: What Children's Minds Tell Us About Truth, Love, and the Meaning of Life.* New York: Farrar, Straus & Giroux, 2009.

Grams, Rollin. "Not 'Leaders' but 'Little Ones' in the Father's Kingdom: The Character of Discipleship in Matthew's gospel." *Transformation* 21/2 (2004) 114–25.

Grunlan, Stephen A. *Marriage and the Family: A Christian Perspective.* Grand Rapids: Zondervan, 1984.

Guijarro, Santiago. "The Family in First-Century Galilee." In *Constructing Early Christian Families: Family as Social Reality and Metaphor*, edited by Halvor Moxnes, 42–65. New York: Routledge, 1997.

Gundry, Judith M. "Children in the Gospel of Mark, with Special Attention to Jesus' Blessing of the Children (Mark 10:13–16) and the Purpose of Mark." In *The Child in the Bible*, edited by Marcia J. Bunge et al., 143–76. Grand Rapids: Eerdmans, 2008.

Gundry-Volf, Judith M. "The Least and the Greatest: Children in the New Testament." In *The Child in Christian Thought*, edited by Marcia Bunge et al., 29–60. Grand Rapids: Eerdmans, 2001.

———. "'To Such as These Belongs the Reign of God': Jesus and Children." *Theology Today* 56/4 (2000) 469–80.

Hamilton, Richard. "Alkman and the Athenian Arkteia." *Hesperia* 58/4 (1989) 449–72.

Bibliography

Hays, Richard B., et al. *Reading the Bible Intertextually*. Waco: Baylor University Press, 2009.

Horn, Cornelia B., and James W. Martens. *"Let the Children Come to Me": Childhood and Children in Early Christianity*. Washington DC: Catholic University of America Press, 2009.

Horsley, Richard A. *Galilee: History, Politics, People*. Valley Forge, PA: Trinity, 1995.

———. *Jesus and the Spiral of Violence: Popular Jewish Resistance in Roman Palestine*. 1st ed. San Francisco: Harper & Row, 1987.

———. *Sociology and the Jesus Movement*. 2nd ed. New York: Continuum, 1994.

Horsley, Richard A., and John S. Hanson. *Bandits, Prophets, and Messiahs: Popular Movements in the Time of Jesus*. Harrisburg, PA: Trinity, 1985.

Jeffers, James S. *The Greco-Roman World of the New Testament Era*. Downers Grove, IL: InterVarsity, 1999.

Jensen, David H. *Graced Vulnerability: A Theology of Childhood*. Cleveland: Pilgrim, 2005.

Johnson, Barbara. "Teaching Deconstructively." In *Writing and Reading Differently: Deconstruction and the Teaching of Composition and Literature*, edited by G. Douglas Atkins and Michael L. Johnson, 140–48. Lawrence, KS: University of Kansas Press, 1985.

Johnson, Luke Timothy. *The Gospel of Luke*. Sacra Pagina 3. Collegeville, MN: Liturgical, 1991.

Jordan, D. R. "A Personal Letter Found in the Athenian Agora." *Hesperia* 69 (2000) 91–103.

Josephus in Nine Volumes. Translated by H. St. J. Thackeray et al. 10 vols. LCL. Cambridge, MA: Harvard University Press, 1926–1965.

Juvenal and Persius. Translated by G. G. Ramsay. LCL. New York: Putnam's Sons, 1924.

Kittel, Gerhard, et al., editors. *Theological Dictionary of the New Testament*. 10 vols. Translated by Geoffrey W. Bromiley. Grand Rapids: Eerdmans, 1964–1976.

Kodell, Jerome. "Luke and the Children: the Beginning and End of the 'Great Interpolation' (Luke 9:46–56, 18:9–23)." *Catholic Biblical Quarterly* 49/3 (1987) 415–30.

Korbin, Jill. "Prologue: A Perspective from Contemporary Childhood Studies." In *Coming of Age in Ancient Greece: Images of Childhood from the Classical Past*, edited by Jenifer Neils and John H. Oakley, 7–13. New Haven: Yale University Press, 2003.

Kovacs, Judith. "Faith and Family in Biblical Perspective." In *Faith and Families*, edited by Lindell Sawyers, 1–39. Philadelphia: Geneva, 1986.

Lacey, Walter Kirkpatrick. *The Family in Classical Greece*. Ithaca: Cornell University Press, 1968.

Lassen, Eva Marie. "The Roman Family: Ideal and Metaphor." In *Constructing Early Christian Families: Family as Social Reality and Metaphor*, edited by Halvor Moxnes, 103–20. New York: Routledge, 1997.

Leaney, Robert. "Jesus and the Symbol of the Child (Luke 9:46–48)." *Expository Times* 66 (1954) 91–92.

Légasse, Simon. *Jésus et l'Enfant: "Enfants," "Petits" et "Simples" dans la tradition synoptique*. Paris: Gabalda, 1969.

Leitch, Vincent B. *Deconstructive Criticism: An Advanced Introduction*. New York: Columbia University Press, 1983.

Liddell, Henry George, and Robert Scott. *A Lexicon, Abridged from Liddell and Scott's Greek-English Lexicon*. Oxford: Clarendon, 1897.

Liebenberg, Jacobus. *The Language of the Kingdom and Jesus: Parable, Aphorism, and Metaphor in the Sayings Material Common to the Synoptic Tradition and the Gospel of Thomas.* Berlin: de Gruyter, 2001.

Liefeld, Walter L. "Luke." In *Zondervan NIV Bible Commentary*, edited by Kenneth L. Barker and John R. Kohlenberger, 2:206–89. Grand Rapids: Zondervan, 1994.

Livy in Fourteen Volumes. Translated by B. O. Foster. LCL. Cambridge, MA: Harvard University Press, 1966.

Lobell, Jarrett A. "Child Burials: Carthage-Tunisia." *Archaeology* 64/1 (2011). Online: http://archive.archaeology.org/1101/topten/tunisia.html.

Lockyer, Herbert. *All the Children of the Bible.* Grand Rapids: Zondervan, 1970.

Lucado, Max. "Fearless Parenting." thrivingfamily.com, November 2010. Online: http://www.thrivingfamily.com/Features/Magazine/2010/nov/fearless-parenting.aspx.

MacDonald, Dennis. *The Homeric Epics and the Gospel of Mark.* New Haven: Yale University Press, 2000.

Malbon, Elizabeth Struthers. *In the Company of Jesus: Characters in Mark's Gospel.* Louisville: Westminster John Knox, 2000.

Malina, Bruce J., and Richard L. Rohrbaugh. *Social Science Commentary on the Synoptic Gospels.* Minneapolis: Fortress, 1992.

Marcus, Joel. *Mark 8–16.* Anchor Yale Bible 27a. New Haven: Yale University Press, 2009.

Martial. *Epigrams.* Translated by Walter C. A. Ker. 2 vols. LCL. Cambridge, MA: Harvard University Press, 1968.

Martin, Luther H. *Hellenistic Religions.* New York: Oxford University Press, 1987.

Martin, Thomas M. *Christian Family Values.* New York: Paulist, 1984.

Martineau, James. *The Bible and the Child: A Discourse.* Boston: Greene, 1845.

Marty, Martin E. *The Mystery of the Child.* Grand Rapids: Eerdmans, 2007.

Mause, Lloyd de, editor. *The History of Childhood.* New York: Psychohistory, 1974.

McCown, Kenneth Jones. "An Outline Study of Child Training According to the Scriptures." MA thesis, Dallas Theological Seminary, 1952.

McGinnis, Claire R. Matthews. "Exodus as a 'Text of Terror' for Children." In *The Child in the Bible*, edited by Marcia J. Bunge et al., 24–44. Grand Rapids: Eerdmans, 2008.

Menander. Translated by W. G. Arnott. Vol. 1. LCL. Cambridge, MA: Harvard University Press, 1977.

Meyers, Carol. "The Family in Early Israel." In *Families in Ancient Israel*, edited by Leo G. Perdue et al., 1–47. Louisville: Westminster John Knox, 1997.

Millen, Rochelle L. *Women, Birth, and Death in Jewish Law and Practice.* Hanover: Brandeis University Press, 2004.

Miller, J. Hillis. "Steven's Rock and Criticism as Cure II." *Georgia Review* 30/2 (1976) 330–48.

Miller, Patrick D. "That the Children May Know: Children in Deuteronomy." In *The Child in the Bible*, edited by Marcia J. Bunge et al., 45–62. Grand Rapids: Eerdmans, 2008.

Miller-McLemore, Bonnie J. "Jesus and the Little Children: An Exercise in the Use of Scripture." Paper presented at the "Children, Youth, and Culture Conference," Austin Presbyterian Theological Seminary, Austin, TX, April 7, 2010.

———. "Jesus Loves the Little Children? An Exercise in the Use of Scripture." *Journal of Childhood and Religion* 1/7 (2010) 1–35.

———. *Let the Children Come: Reimagining Childhood from a Christian Perspective.* Families and Faith. San Francisco: Jossey-Bass, 2003.

Miscall, Peter D. "Isaiah: New Heavens, New Earth, New Book." In *Reading Between Texts: Intertextuality and the Hebrew Bible*, edited by Danna N. Fewell, 41–56. Louisville: Westminster John Knox, 1992.

Moxnes, Halvor. "What is Family? Problems in constructing early Christian families." In *Constructing Early Christian Families: Family as Social Reality and Metaphor*, edited by Halvor Moxnes, 13–41. New York: Routledge, 1997.

Müller, Peter. *In der Mitte der Gemeinde: Kinder im Neuen Testament*. Neukirchen-Vluyn: Neukirchener, 1992.

———. "Die Metapher vom 'Kind Gottes' und die neutestamentliche Theologie." In *". . .Was ihr auf dem Weg verhandelt habt": Beiträge zur Exegese und Theologie des Neuen Testaments: Festschrift für Ferdinand Hahn zum 75. Geburtstag*, edited by Peter Müller et al., 192–203. Neukirchen-Vluyn: Neukirchener, 2001.

———. "Gottes Kinder. Zur Metaphorik der Gotteskindschaft im Neuen Testament." *Jahrbuch für biblische Theologie* 17 (2002) 141–62.

Murphy, A. James. "Family Values: Anti-Familial Rhetoric and Counterculture in the Sayings of Jesus, a Social-Structural Study." MA thesis, Missouri State University, May 2001.

———. "Ignoring Women: Exclusion of the Female from Divine Communication in Leviticus." Unpublished paper presented to the faculty of the Iliff School of Theology, March 2007.

———. "Children in Deuteronomy: The Partisan Nature of Divine Justice." *Biblical Interpretation* 20 (2012) 1–15.

———. Review of *The Child in the Bible*, by Marcia J. Bunge et al., editors. *Journal of Childhood and Religion* 1 (2010) 1–9. Online: http://www.childhoodandreligion. com/JCR_Book_Reviews_files/Bunge%20review.pdf.

Myers, Ched. "As a Child: Jesus' Solidarity with the Least of the Least." *Living Pulpit* 12/4 (2003) 18–19, 33.

———. *Binding the Strongman: A Political Reading of Mark's Story of Jesus*. Maryknoll, NY: Orbis, 1988.

Mylonas, George. "Eleusis and the Eleusinian Mysteries." *Classical Journal* 43/3 (1947) 131–46.

Newman, Barclay Moon, editor. *Concise Greek-English Dictionary of the New Testament*. Stuttgart: Deutsche Bibelgesellschaft, 1993.

Neyrey, Jerome H. *Honor and Shame in the Gospel of Matthew*. Louisville: Westminster John Knox, 1998.

Niels, Jennifer and John H. Oakley, editors. *Coming of Age in Ancient Greece: Images of Childhood from the Classical Past*. New Haven: Yale University Press, 2003.

Nkwoka, Anthony. "Mark 10:13–16: Jesus' Attitude to Children and its Modern Challenges." *Africa Theological Journal* 14/2 (1985) 100–110.

Osiek, Carolyn, and David L. Balch. *Families in the New Testament World: Households and House Churches*. Edited by Don S. Browning, and Ian S. Evison Browning. 1st ed. Family, Religion, and Culture. Louisville: Westminster John Knox, 1997.

Ostmeyer, Karl-Heinrich. "Jesu Annahme der Kinder in Matthäus 19:13–15." *Novum Testamentum* 46/1 (2004) 1–11.

Ovid in six volumes. Vols. 3–4, *Metamorphoses*. Cambridge, MA: Harvard University Press, 1975.

Pausanias. *Description of Greece*. Translated by W. H. S. Jones. 5 vols. LCL. Cambridge, MA: Harvard University Press, 1977.

Patte, Daniel. "Jesus' Pronouncement about Entering the Kingdom like a Child: A Structural Exegesis." *Semeia* 29 (1983) 3–42

Penner, James A. "Revelation and Discipleship in Matthew's Transfiguration Account." *Bibliotheca Sacra* 152 (1995) 201–10.

Perdue, Leo G. "The Israelite and Early Jewish Family." In *Families in Ancient Israel*, edited by Leo G. Perdue et al., 163–222. Louisville: Westminster John Knox, 1997.

Perkins, Pheme. *Mark.* New Interpreter's Bible 8. Nashville: Abingdon, 1996.

Petronius. Edited by E. H. Warmington. Translated by Michael Heseltine. 1st rev. ed. Cambridge, MA: Harvard University Press, 1975.

Philo in Ten Volumes (and Two Supplementary Volumes). Translated by F. H. Colson. LCL. Cambridge, MA: Harvard University Press,

Pilch, John J. "'Beat His Ribs While He is Young' (Sir 30:12) A Window on the Mediterranean World." *Biblical Theology Bulletin* 23/3 (1993) 101–13.

Plato. *Plato in Twelve Volumes.* Vol. 7. Translated by H. N. Fowler. LCL. Cambridge, MA: Harvard University Press, 1975–1984.

Plautus. Translated by Paul Nixon. 5 vols. LCL. Cambridge, MA: Harvard University Press, 1965.

Pliny. *Letters and Panegyricus.* Translated by Betty Radice. 2 vols. LCL. Cambridge, MA: Harvard University Press, 1969.

Plutarch's Lives in Eleven Volumes. Translated by Bernadotte Perrin. LCL. Cambridge, MA: Harvard University Press, 1969–1982.

Plutarch's Moralia in Sixteen Volumes. Translated by F.C. Babbitt. LCL. Cambridge, MA: Harvard University Press, 1967–1984.

Pollock, Linda A. *Forgotten Children: Parent-Child Relations from 1500–1900.* Cambridge: Cambridge University Press, 1983.

Pomeroy, Arthur J. "Trimalchio as *Deliciae*." *Phoenix* 46 (1992) 45–53.

Pridmore, John S. *The New Testament Theology of Childhood.* Hobart, Tasmania: Buckland, 1977.

Quintilian. *The Institutio Oratoria of Quintilian in Four Volumes.* Translated by H. E. Butler. New York: Putnam's Sons, 1921.

Raedts, Peter. "The Children's Crusade of 1212." *Journal of Medieval History* 3 (1977) 279–324.

Rawson, Beryl, "Adult-Child Relationships in Roman Society." In *Marriage, Divorce, and Children in Ancient Rome*, edited by Beryl Rawson, 1–30. Canberra: Humanities Research Centre, 1991.

———. "Children in the Roman *Familia*." In *The Family in Ancient Rome: New Perspectives*, edited by Beryl Rawson, 170–200. Ithaca: Cornell University Press, 1986.

Rawson, Beryl, editor. *The Family in Ancient Rome: New Perspectives.* Ithaca: Cornell University Press, 1986.

———. *Marriage, Divorce, and Children in Ancient Rome.* Canberra: Humanities Research Centre, 1991.

Reinhartz, Adele. "Parents and Children: A Philonic Perspective." In *The Jewish Family in Antiquity*, edited by Shaye J. D. Cohen, 61–88. Brown Judaic Studies 289. Atlanta: Scholars, 1993.

Robbins, Vernon K. "Pronouncement Stories and Jesus' Blessing of Children." *Semeia* 29 (1983) 43–74.

Rose, H. J. *Ancient Roman Religion.* London: Hutchinson's University Library, 1948.

Safrai, S. *The Jewish People in the First Century*. Edited by S. Safrai and M. Stern. 2 vols. Philadelphia: Fortress, 1976.

Saller, Richard. "Corporeal Punishment, Authority, and Obedience in the Roman Household." In *Marriage, Divorce, and Children in Ancient Rome*, edited by Beryl Rawson, 144–65. Canberra: Humanities Research Centre, 1991.

Schilling, F. A. "What Means the Saying about Receiving the Kingdom of God as a Little Child?" *Expository Times* 77 (1965–1966) 56–58.

Schneemelcher, Wilhelm, editor. *New Testament Apocrypha* Vols. 1–2. Rev. ed. Louisville: Westminster John Knox, 1991–1992.

Schofield, Alison. *From Qumran to the Yahad: A New Paradigm of Textual Development for the Community Rule*. Leiden: Brill, 2009.

Select Papyri. Vol. 1, *Non-literary Papyri: Private Affairs*. Translated by A. S. Hunt and C. C. Edgar. LCL. Cambridge, MA: Harvard University Press, 1970.

Seneca, Lucius Annaeus. *Seneca in Ten Volumes. Moral Essays*. Translated by John W. Basore in Three Volumes. LCL. Cambridge, MA: Harvard University Press, 1968–1979.

Shelley, Dennis D. "An Exegetical Study of Matthew 18:1–14, and its Relationship to Child Evangelism." MA thesis, Capital Bible Seminary, 1977.

Sim, David C. "What about the Wives and Children of the Disciples? The Cost of Discipleship from another perspective." *Heythrop Journal* 35 (1994) 373–90.

Stambaugh, John E., and David L. Balch. *The New Testament in Its Social Environment*. Philadelphia: Westminster, 1986.

Strange, William A. *Children in the Early Church*. Cumbria, UK: Paternoster, 1996.

Suetonius. Translated by J. C. Rolfe. 2 vols. LCL. Cambridge, MA: Harvard University Press, 1979.

Tacitus, Cornelius. *The Histories and the Annals*. Translated by C. H. Moore and J. Jackson. 4 vols. LCL. Cambridge, MA: Harvard University Press, 1937.

Taylor-Wingender, Paulette. "Kids of the Kingdom (a Study of Matthew 18:1–5 and its Context)." *Direction* 17/2 (1988) 18–25.

Thaden, Robert H. von. "Thinking with Children: Children as Conceptual Characters in Wisdom Traditions." Paper presented at the annual meeting of the Society of Biblical Literature, Boston. November 2008.

Thatcher, Adrian. "Beginning Again with Jesus." In *Children's Voices: Children's Perspectives in Ethics, Theology and Religious Education*, edited by A. Dillen and D. Pollefeyt, 137–63. Leuven: Peeters, 2010.

Theissen, Gerd. "Itinerant Radicalism: The Tradition of Jesus Sayings from the Perspective of the Sociology of Literature." In *The Bible and Liberation: A Radical Religion Reader*, edited by The Radical Religion Collective, 84–93. Berkeley: Community for Religious Research and Education, 1976.

———. *Sociology of Early Palestinian Christianity*. Philadelphia: Fortress, 1978.

———. "Wanderradikalismus: Literatursoziologische Aspekte der Überlieferung von Worten Jesu im Urchristentum." *Zeitschrift für Theologie und Kirche* 70 (1973) 245–71.

Thompson, Marianne Meye. "Children in the Gospel of John." In *The Child in the Bible*, edited by Marcia J. Bunge et al., 195–214. Grand Rapids: Eerdmans, 2008.

Todd, Emmanuel. *The Explanation of Ideology: Family Structure and Social Systems*. Translated by David Garrioch. Oxford: Blackwell, 1989.

Towner, W. Sibley. "Children in the Image of God." In *The Child in the Bible*, edited by Marcia J. Bunge et al., 307–23. Grand Rapids: Eerdmans, 2008.

UNICEF. "Child Trafficking." Online: http://www.unicef.org/protection/57929_58005.html.

Weber, Hans-Ruedi. *Jesus and the Children: Biblical Resources for Study and Preaching.* Atlanta: Knox, 1979.

———. "The Gospel in the Child." *Ecumenical Review* 31/3 (1979) 227–33.

White, Keith J. "'He Placed a Little Child in the Midst': Jesus, the Kingdom, and Children." In *The Child in the Bible*, edited by Marcia J. Bunge et al., 353–74. Grand Rapids: Eerdmans, 2008.

Yancey, Philip. *Where is God When It Hurts?* Grand Rapids: Zondervan, 1997.

Xenophon. *Oeconomicus.* Translated by Sarah B. Pomeroy. Oxford: Clarendon, 1994.

Yarbrough, O. Larry. "Parents and Children in the Jewish Family of Antiquity." In *The Jewish Family in Antiquity*, edited by Shaye J. D. Cohen, 39–60. Brown Judaic Studies 289. Atlanta: Scholars, 1993.